American Academy of Political and Social Science

The foreign Policy of the United States

Political and Commercial

American Academy of Political and Social Science

The foreign Policy of the United States
Political and Commercial

ISBN/EAN: 9783337133252

Printed in Europe, USA, Canada, Australia, Japan

Cover: Foto ©ninafisch / pixelio.de

More available books at **www.hansebooks.com**

SUPPLEMENT TO THE
ANNALS OF THE AMERICAN ACADEMY OF POLITICAL AND SOCIAL SCIENCE.
MAY, 1899.

The Foreign Policy

OF THE

United States:

Political and Commercial.

Addresses and Discussion at the Annual Meeting of the American Academy of Political and Social Science, April 7-8, 1899.

PHILADELPHIA:
AMERICAN ACADEMY OF POLITICAL AND SOCIAL SCIENCE.
1899.

CONTENTS.

	PAGE
THE GOVERNMENT OF DEPENDENCIES.	
Addresses:	
Theodore S. Woolsey, Yale University	3
E. W. Huffcut, Cornell University	19
A Lawrence Lowell, Harvard University	46
W. Alleyne Ireland, London	60
Discussion:	
Talcott Williams, Philadelphia	65
Leo S. Rowe, University of Pennsylvania	70
MILITARISM AND DEMOCRACY.	
Address: Carl Schurz	77
COMMERCIAL RELATIONS OF THE UNITED STATES WITH THE FAR EAST.	
Addresses:	
Worthington C. Ford, Boston	107
Robert T. Hill, Washington	131
Discussion:	
John Foord, New York	144
William P. Wilson, Philadelphia	154
Emory R. Johnson, University of Pennsylvania	158
THE POLITICAL RELATIONS OF THE UNITED STATES WITH THE FAR EAST.	
Addresses:	
John Bassett Moore, Columbia University	163
His Excellency Wu Ting-fang	168
Discussion:	
Lindley M. Keasbey, Bryn Mawr College	177
Frederick W. Williams, Yale University	184

APPENDICES

I. REPORT OF ANNUAL MEETING	201
II. INTRODUCTORY ADDRESSES OF THE PRESIDENT, PROFESSOR EDMUND J. JAMES.	
The Academy and its Work	205
Introducing Hon. Carl Schurz	212
The East and the West	215

The Government of Dependencies.

Addresses and Discussions.

THE GOVERNMENT OF DEPENDENCIES.

THEODORE S. WOOLSEY, *Professor of International Law,
Yale University.*

In every state with colonies, its government of them must depend upon two factors: (1) the prevailing theory of the dependent relation; (2) the constitutional limitations, if any, under which it lives. There are two theories to define the relationship between a state and its dependencies. One considers them property from which an income is to be drawn; the other considers them a kind of trust, to be administered for the benefit of their inhabitants.

A good example of the first is the Dutch rule in Java. The Javanese number approximately twenty-five millions. They are governed by two-fifths of one per cent of their number of Europeans. The island is considered a sort of huge farm by the government of the Netherlands. The method of administration, called the "culture system," is one of forced labor. Introduced in 1830, under the influence of a more enlightened public sentiment it is now disappearing. At times it has paid a surplus as high as ten million dollars into the Dutch treasury: but this has given place to a deficit. Under it, the Dutch government discouraged European immigration, education and missionary labor. There was no autonomy. Generally speaking there was no private property. And the result was that the natives deteriorated in artistic, industrial and scientific processes.

If we look for examples of the other, the trust theory, we shall find a very general opinion that the British system is best worth copying. During the second quarter of the present century, Great Britain finally gave her various dependencies self-government, unrestricted trade and reform administrations, wherever practicable. In those climates where the white man can work and multiply, in Canada, Australia and New Zealand for instance, self-governing colonies have been developed, with large liberty of action, duties to protect domestic manufactures against British competition having even been permitted. In the minor colonies of the temperate zone, and in the tropics, where dependencies have been retained in the hands of the crown, the principle of self-sacrifice has still prevailed, and the results have justified it. For we find, on the whole, prosperity, contentment and loyalty. A blind attachment to the opposite theory has cost Spain her colonies, and makes those of France, in the opinion of enlightened Frenchmen like M. Hanotaux and M. Leroy-Beaulieu, a failure. Now under the system of Great Britain, she spends and her colonies do not contribute; she protects and they enjoy. A judge of the High Court of Calcutta, Mr. Cunningham, wrote in 1882, "we have definitely abandoned the idea that the political connection of England and India can be a source of direct gain to any public body or to the English nation."

Where, then, does the profit of a state in the matter of dependencies come in? It comes from the enlarged opportunity for the energies of its surplus youth, and in that stimulated trade which follows the flag. This is peculiarly true in the case of Great Britain. Her narrow limits at home offer but restricted opportunity for business and agricultural activities; while, on the other hand, her long supremacy in manufactures of certain kinds and her control of the carrying trade, enable her to take peculiar advantage of the traffic with her dependencies, by which example other nations like Germany have been tempted, to their hurt.

When we are forced by circumstances to study a form of government for our own dependencies, we turn naturally, therefore, to those British territories which most resemble them, and seek to learn the secret of their success or the warning in their failure.

My subject in terms is general, relating to the government of all dependencies. I shall take the liberty of making it more specific, the government of our own. These are of two classes, those which are placed under our sovereignty and those which are placed under our protection. In the latter class is Cuba. By treaty Spain has relinquished her sovereignty in Cuba. She does not cede it to us; she simply lets it go, reciting the fact that the island is "to be occupied" by the United States. The result of this must be that the sovereignty remains in abeyance with reversion to the Cubans themselves. Spain recognizes our assumption of responsibility for Cuba's actions, until we are satisfied of its "pacification." To secure this was our avowed object in waging war; everything else which has been won, was an accident. To correspond to this responsibility and to enable us to make it good, we must have a certain power. This in Cuba's foreign relations is exclusive; in her domestic concerns it must be so shared between the Cubans and ourselves as to give them that degree of autonomy which will fit them for eventual independence (either in our Union or separately), while retaining control enough to be correlative with our liabilities. Our first step very properly consists in military occupation, using our soldiers as a constabulary. This means order and better sanitation and protection to local industries and the revival throughout the length and breadth of the island, of all the arts of peace. To accomplish the desired end, this must be accompanied by the gradual resumption of civil government in all the municipalities, and by the formation of an island legislature to control internal affairs, subject to the veto of the United States representative.

All franchises should be in the hands of the native local authorities; the execution of the laws should be entrusted to native elected officers; the courts to judge causes under the local law should be Cuban also. We protect Cuba from outside aggression, and by veto from her own inexperience and folly, and prevent acts of hostility to ourselves. But the revenues of the island, after paying for the maintenance of our soldiers so long as they are necessary and of our few necessary officials, must be spent for her own benefit. This is a protectorate. Whether the issue of the protectorate is independence, or, as many believe, annexation, the process of education, of pacification, is the same. It consists, in a word, in granting as much control over internal affairs as the inhabitants are able to bear. And we must so regulate their duties and revenue laws and commercial rights, as to give them a prosperous life, even at our own cost, that is, if we wish the experiment to turn out well. Thus we should open the door to foreign trade on as favorable terms as to our own. Instead of regarding the traffic between Cuba and the states as coasting trade, we should open it to foreign ships. And between Spaniards and Cubans, we should not discriminate.

All this we can properly and lawfully do, because we have not assumed the Cuban's sovereignty; so far as they are concerned we are not tied down by our constitution. Here we see the difference between protected and ceded territory. In the cases of Porto Rico and the Philippines, we are under constitutional limitations. Here there is no presumption of future independence. They are our spoils of war, to govern as Spain did, or to govern as Great Britain would, so far as our constitution allows. All depends upon the kind of results we desire. Some government we must provide, nor is it clear that this task will be easily shifted to other shoulders. While the ratification of the peace treaty was still an open question, it was urged that this step committed the United States to nothing; that in the Philippines at least, cession would give place in time to a protectorate or a sale or the establishment of a republic. I do not think we should shirk the question of a permanent government for them, under any such illusion. Anything other than permanent possession, however desirable, will be most difficult. My reasons for this view are, first, that future surrender is sure to be construed as a confession of failure, and would hurt the national pride. We need not have assumed the burden, but having done so, it must be patiently and loyally borne. Then, too, it will be much less easy to relinquish sovereignty than it was to refuse it. It implies the favorable conjunction of three bodies, two legislative, one executive, against in the latter case one-third of the Senate. And lastly, the whole spirit and tendency of the European policy which we are following, forbids such surrender. It strengthens the loose tie, rather than loosens the strong one. France in Madagascar, converting a protectorate into a colony, and England in Egypt, only awaiting the right moment to make her own that territory which she has repeatedly promised to evacuate, are examples of this.

To return from this digression.

Between Porto Rico and the Philippines, both now equally under the sovereignty of the United States, there is a gulf fixed, climatic, social, racial, as well as geographical. In Porto Rico we find a settled society largely of European stock; law-abiding, fairly prosperous, in a healthful climate where our race can live and work, and whither it is likely to migrate until the opportunities are filled. Here are materials for a state after territorial apprenticeship. Or as an unorganized territory, we may watch it working out its ideas of self-government. For, when Congress sees fit to legislate, the government of Porto Rico should be laid as largely as possible upon the shoulders of its own people. Military rule should not be necessary, and a carpet-bag system would produce results which we can pretty definitely forecast. Native officials, a native legislature, the existing laws and municipal regulations should be the starting point. Upon the present system should gradually be engrafted those changes which reason and experience, theirs and ours, may suggest, and which Spain has heretofore prevented. There will be difficulties, there may be failure, but both are a means of education. And education in the art of self-government, is what we aim at giving, unless our policy and our professions are alike disregarded.

The case of the Philippines stands on a far different footing. Cuba and Porto Rico are near our shores; the Philippines are far away. The first have long been within our sphere of influence; possession of the second, suddenly makes us an Asiatic power, and thrusts us without warning into the political and commercial melting pot of the Orient. The first are in the main civilized; the second on the whole savage. In the first, white men can live and work; in the second they can only make others work. The capacity for self-government may exist in the one, but not so clearly in the other. We may govern the one by reason; for the other we shall need force. Porto Rico will pay its own way. The Philippines are certain to be a heavy burden. These are some of the reasons which made the cession of the Philippines a vulnerable point in the peace treaty. That treaty is now ratified, and we must make the best of it.

I say nothing about the administration of Hawaii, for that is being laid down by Congress. I assume moreover that the Aguinaldo insurrection will be soon put down and the island of Luzon pacified. It is the next step, the government after order is restored, which is the crux of the whole problem.

And here our minds naturally turn to India. The British rule in India is based upon conquest and maintained by force. By war the limits of dominion are constantly being extended. To justify the mastery of many millions of people by a handful of alien conquerors, has required generations of honest administration, giving continuous proof of altruistic effort. The governing class has wisely pursued a policy of indifferentism in the matter of religion, neither discriminating between beliefs already embraced, nor seeking to propagate its own. So far as practicable it has sought to administer elementary justice through native officials, whose ability is tested by competitive examination. The covenanted civil service is open to British youth by competition, with tenure of office during good behavior, promotion in reserve and a handsome retiring pension in the background. It is a picked class, drawn from the flower of the race, with public school training behind it, and animated by a strong preference for the administrative, not the commercial career. It makes a study, a science, of the business of governing dependent races, and the result is a commendable *esprit de corps*. All of this is the consequence of historical development, nor has this ceased. Thus at present the benevolent despotism of the last generation seems to be giving place to a stricter adherence to legal forms. Complaint is made that promotion goes too much by seniority, taking too little account of proved capacity. The fall in the silver rupee, in which the covenanted receive pay, has made the service less desirable. Some of the commissionerships are too large and unwieldy for one man and should be divided. These are criticisms, but as things are, the competition is still keen and the class secured good.

At the head of the government stands the Secretary of State for India, guided by a Council and sitting in London. Next comes the Governor-General, commonly but not officially known as Viceroy, with an Executive Council made up of heads of departments, the Viceroy taking that of foreign affairs. This Council is enlarged into a legislative council by the addition of the Governor of that province in which it is held, of official delegates from Madras and Bombay, and of certain non-official representatives of European and of native communities. Then come the governors of the two presidencies, also with councils; the lieutenant-governors of Bengal, the Punjab and the Northwestern Provinces; the chief commissioners of other provinces, together forming a class subordinate to the Viceroy.

Under these are the 238 districts, grouped into commissionerships, their heads being called collector magistrates or deputy-commissioners. These are both fiscal and judicial officers, but concern themselves also with everything under the sun, from police to agriculture, from road-making to the social life of the people. For they are " the representatives of a paternal, not a constitutional government."*

The districts containing an average of over 800,000 people, are in turn subdivided, this being the final unit of administration. The laws enforced are British acts, Indian Council enactments, native laws and native customs. The judicial jurisdiction corresponds largely to the magisterial and fiscal, and one of the curious features is the frequent union of two out of the three characters in the same person. A soldier also is sometimes made a district officer.

Each province has its own judicial system, with a chain of authorities ending in the High Court, and to this law, so interpreted, all alike are subject. The characteristics of the whole system appear to be, paternalism, comprehensiveness, justice and order. The great majority of the minor civil offices are filled by natives; the higher judges are mostly European. Indeed the suggestion to place non-official Europeans under the jurisdiction of any natives created a tempest of opposition.

The results of British administration in India have been splendid. It has kept the peace, preserved order, built roads, railroads and irrigation works, brought justice to the humblest, lessened famine and pestilence, introduced state education, sanitation and dispensaries, freed trade from many burdens, simplified taxation, and has begun to introduce local self-government. A single detail further is pertinent. The imperial revenue is drawn chiefly from salt and opium monopolies and from the land tax; its expenditure, excluding capital or construction account, is about equal to its income.

* Encyc. Brit., Art. India, p. 769, ninth ed.

Now very much of this system, particularly its basic ideas, will repay our study in considering the Philippines. We must practice religious toleration toward Christian and Mohammedan alike, even to the limit of indifferentism, yet not protecting abuses. We must keep a firm hand on the so-called civilized natives, who constitute one-half of the population, and yet educate them to some measure of local administration which they can in time undertake themselves. We must better communications and build public works. We must raise revenue skillfully and spend it more and more on the country. We must get work out of an indolent race, without slavery or its equivalent in contract labor, probably by introducing it to new wants. Life is necessarily indolent, where existence is so ridiculously easy. We must guide the savage half with the strength which he will respect and the courage which he will admire. Justice and good faith are essential in dealing with both classes: justice, inexpensive, swift and incorruptible, administered by a permanent trained service with higher ideals than personal advantage. All of this is suggested by the British rule in India; it is essential to success; how can it be made practicable? Here we come in sight of our constitutional limitations, for it is the merest folly to trace out an ideal course and laugh away the obstacles.

Let us assume that the United States may acquire territory, when and how it chooses. Let us grant that there is no obligation, either now or in the remote future, to form this territory into states. Nevertheless the moment Congress begins to legislate for the Philippines and establishes there civil government, whether on the lines above indicated or on any others, that moment the constitutional guarantees begin to work. This was the case in the unorganized territory of Alaska. In accordance with these guarantees, though a legislative assembly and a delegate to Congress are prohibited, the rights of habeas corpus and of a jury trial are recognized, by statute.*

* 23 U. S. Stats. pp. 24-27.

These personal guarantees are contained in the body of the constitution and its amendments. They relate in general to the security of life, liberty and property. They include specifically religious freedom; free speech and a free press; the right of assembling and of petition; the right to bear arms; security from unreasonable search and seizure; freedom from the quartering of troops; the necessity of presentment by a grand jury on a capital charge; the right of compulsory process to secure witnesses; the aid of counsel when accused; above all the right of trial by jury.

It is to be noted that some of these provisions are by nature or in terms applicable to all the territory of the United States, while others, being civil rather than political rights, may be capable of limitation to the citizens of the states and their grantees under title of the people of the United States. This distinction is by no means certain: it is merely a possible loophole of escape, if the supreme court should be urged to deny the Philippines certain inconvenient rights, that to bear arms, for instance.

But in order to stand on the safest possible ground let me place together here the guarantees concerning whose extension to all United States terrritory there can be little question.

First comes the right of trial by jury.

This is contained in the final clause of Section 2, Article III, as follows: "The trial of all crimes, except in cases of impeachment, shall be by jury; and such trial shall be held in the state where the said crimes shall have been committed; but when not committed within any state the trial shall be at such place or places as the Congress may by law have directed." This language is pretty clear, but by judicial construction it has been made still clearer.* In an illuminating and most judicial article upon the constitutional questions incident to the acquisition and government of

---

*Callan v. Wilson, 127 U. S., 540, 550; Thompson v. Utah, 170 U. S., 343, 346. See also Am. Publ. Co. v. Fisher, 166 U. S., 464, 466.

island territory by the United States (Harv. Law Rev., XII, No. 6), Judge Baldwin examines the origin of this jury trial provision, its phrasing, and its construction by the supreme court. He expresses the belief that unless the views of that court should be overruled, "they must lead to the conclusion that no conviction for crime could be had in any of our new possessions, after the establishment there of an orderly civil government, except upon a jury trial."

On the same plane with the right of trial by jury stand those guarantees, contained in the amendments to the constitution, which are neither inserted specifically for the benefit of the "people" of the United States, nor relate to rights merely political. Those most germane to our topic are here enumerated:

Slavery is forbidden in the United States "or any place subject to their jurisdiction."

Religious liberty is provided.

Indictment by a grand jury is necessary to a trial for an infamous crime.

No man can be compelled to give testimony against himself.

No person can be deprived of life, liberty or property without due process of law.

No cruel or unusual punishment may be inflicted.

If now these constitutional rights relating to persons and property extend to all the territories of the United States, they must exist in the Philippines, and must be taken account of in the question of governing the Philippines. The inhabitants of these islands are thought to number from eight to ten millions, of eighty distinct tribes which are classified by Professor Worcester as Negritos (the descendants of the aborigines), Mohammedan Malays, Pagan Malays, and civilized Malays, the latter being one-half of the whole. These domesticated Malays are described as fairly intelligent, but dishonest, untruthful, and so indolent that crops spoil for lack of laborers.

Foreman, who had much fuller information than Worcester, and is the authority upon whom Worcester largely relies, gives a curious list of their virtues and vices, and confesses that he cannot understand their character. It is a succession of surprises, he says. They are hospitable, cleanly, sober and patient; they are incapable of gratitude, profligate, undependable, improvident, cruel, impertinent, superstitious, treacherous. The few in the cities imitate European usages; the many regard the European as a demoniacal being, or at least an enemy. All are liars, even in the confessional. " The native is so contumacious to all bidding," writes Foreman, " so averse to social order, that he can only be ruled by coercion, by the demonstration of force."

There is reason for this judgment. Of sixty-six provinces, nineteen under Spanish rule had a civil governor, forty-seven a military one; yet the civil governor was the head of carbineers and police, of the departments of education, prisons, health, works, forests, mines, agriculture, mails, telegraph; in charge of everything but the public funds, so that he could not have fallen far behind his military colleague as a reservoir of force.

Such are the domesticated half. The savage half range between docility and ferocity, between innocency and piracy, many tribes having never yielded to the Spaniard.

Now if we place such people as these in possession of such constitutional rights as those mentioned, we have a *reductio ad absurdum*. How can we establish over them a civil government which would be anything but a mockery, if we must concede indictment by grand jury for *some* crimes and trial by jury for *all?* It would mean the breakdown of any criminal system to which it was applied and unchecked crime means administrative failure. And in addition, unless by construction the other guarantees could be put out of reach, like edged tools rescued from children's hands, we might have to concede the right to bear arms to persons intending assassination; a free press, although teaching open sedition; the right of assembling when it endangered our sovereignty.*

As Judge Baldwin well says, to give half-civilized peoples the benefit of immunities framed by a civilized people for itself "would be a serious obstacle to the maintenance there of an efficient government. Every people under a written constitution must experience difficulties of administration that are unknown to nations like Great Britain which are unfettered by legal restraints imposed by former generations. It is part of the price that it pays for liberty, that new conditions must be dealt with in fundamentals, under old laws."

Nevertheless we need not despair of our ability to frame a suitable government for the Philippines, even if, as I believe, a civil government, under our constitution, is and must be for the indefinite future, inadmissible. We have still the military solution in reserve, and to that we have recourse by process of exclusion.

Govern we must. Civil government would mean chaos, if the personal guarantees go with it. No government can succeed there which is not based upon force. We need to place a benevolent despot in every district in the Archipelago. Therefore the military government is the only one possible. And this is dependent upon the inaction of Congress. Its constitutional basis lies in the fact that the United States as sovereign is responsible for the maintenance of justice and order, for the defence of its territory, for the protection of its subjects' rights. This duty is in the hands of Congress as part of its general rights, and also under the "needful rules and regulations" clause, regarding territory. Pending action by Congress, this duty devolves upon the President, the Executive

---

* In Mormon Ch. v. U. S. (136 U. S. 44) Mr. Justice Bradley said for the Court, "Doubtless Congress in legislating for the territories would be subject to those fundamental limitations in favor of personal rights, which are formulated in the Constitution and its amendments; but these limitations would exist rather by inference and the general spirit of the Constitution from which Congress derives all its powers, than by any express and direct application of its provisions."

head of the nation and Commander-in-Chief of both army and navy. The law applicable would not be martial law, for that implies war, or insurgency; it would not be military law except as to the discipline of the army itself; it would be simply the will of the President, but expressed so far as practicable in terms of the law already existing, and executed by the President's representatives, the officers of the United States army. This despotic form of administration is not an ideal method; its justification is that no other is practicable.

In using the army officers for administrative work, we should be doing nothing new. The first act relating to Louisiana, in 1803, empowered the President to appoint all civil, military and judicial officers of the new territory, define their duties and support them with the army and navy. "It was in effect the establishment of a military despotism over Louisiana, and may suffice as an example of the extent to which the sovereign power of the United States over territories might go, if a wiser policy were not the rule," writes Alexander Johnston. The untaxed Indians, who are expressly excluded from the right of representation, have at times been cared for by our army officers acting as agents, and with a success in agreeable contrast to that of the average Indian agent.

There are two qualities among many, which the history of the British in India emphasizes as peculiarly desirable in those persons who have to govern dependent peoples. One is physical strength and courage; the other a high sense of honor. Those splendid men who saved India in the Mutiny, men both in the civil and military service, the two Lawrences, Edwards, Neville Chamberlain, Roberts, John Nicholson and many like them, may well serve as examples of the value of these qualities. Their courage and vigor won the native admiration; their honorable dealing won confidence and love. The relationship between governor and governed is a fiduciary one, like that between guardian and ward. Its basis must be the sense of honor. Now is it not more likely that we shall find the union of these two qualities in our army officers of West Point training, than amongst any other class of citizens available for such work? They are taught both to obey and to command. They are picked men, physically. Honor is the basis of the army organization, for conduct unbecoming an officer and a gentleman costs a man his commission. Just so far as the influence of politics and of politicians can be excluded, the regular army is to be trusted. We must use it to obtain order; I believe that we can and must use it also to maintain order and administer justice.

There will be difficulties in the way. One will be the status of foreigners in the Philippines. We cannot grant them exterritorial privileges, for that would be inconsistent with our dignity; nor can we deny them civil rights, particularly when specified by treaty with their country; our own citizens would be likewise in a false position. Some makeshift would be required, like a plaster to a sore spot, for instance the application of the laws of Oregon and a Federal Court to others than natives. Another difficulty may arise from the religious orders. These friars serve as parish priests; they are large holders of property; this property is secured to them under the terms of the Spanish treaty, preventing sequestration; the educational system, such as it is, is in their hands. In Spanish times the church constantly intrigued against any governor who preferred the interests of the state to its own, and this same spirit, perhaps stirring up native opposition, we must expect to encounter.

Then there is the raising of revenue. Under Spanish rule, the larger items of income came from fifteen days' forced labor per head, per annum, or its commutation, five million dollars and over; from customs, two millions; from government monopolies, stamps, gambling, opium, cock-fighting, and so on, one million; from lotteries, one-half million.

Much of this is not a proper source of revenue for an enlightened nation. Even with these illegitimate sources of income, Spain made a deficit. "There is no record," writes Foreman, "that the Philippines have ever been in a flourishing financial condition."

Lastly, there is always the chance that Congress, in order to embarrass a president of a different political complexion, may decide to embark upon civil government, and take this tremendous, perhaps dangerous, despotic power out of the Executive's hands.

So that we can hardly expect plain sailing. Our duty is to respect the Constitution, patiently and loyally to do our best under the circumstances, and then to "wish for the day."

CONSTITUTIONAL ASPECTS OF THE GOVERNMENT OF DEPENDENCIES.

E. W. HUFFCUT, *Professor of Law, Cornell University.*

With the acquisition of Hawaii, Porto Rico and the Philippines, three novel and interesting problems in the government of dependencies confront the United States. First, we are called upon to govern what yesterday was a white man's oligarchy, resting upon the ruins of a semi-savage monarchy, with a basis of native Pacific islanders, a stratum of Japanese and Chinese, another of Portuguese, and an upper crust of domiciled Americans and Englishmen and Germans. Second, we are called upon to govern an ancient Spanish colony, densely populated, with a proud and impatient Latin race as the dominant factor. Third, we are called upon to govern an ancient Spanish satrapy, densely populated with native islanders of varying races, in varying stages of development, and lying in tropical latitudes alleged to be unfit for Caucasian colonization.

In some respects the problems are totally different from those which have confronted any other government in its dealings with dependencies. Even Hawaii, least difficult of all the problems, presents some novel features, as, for example, the presence of so large a body of subjects of foreign states as to whom our policy has been one of exclusion. Porto Rico, on the other hand, presents to us the difficult task of reconciling an influential class of intelligent Europeans to a change of rulers, of educating the Spaniards, bred in the habits of political thought common to the Latin races, to the notions underlying the American form of government, and, at the same time, preserving the distinctions between the independent form of government of our states and organized territories and that necessary for a dependent outlying island possession. I am not sure but this is, after all, our hardest problem. Whether it is or not must depend upon the attitude of the dominant class in the island. As to the Philippines, I content myself with quoting from the Hon. James Bryce (*Century Magazine*, March 1899, p. 726): " Probably no task has been presented to the English in India or in any of their colonies during the last fifty years so difficult as that to which Americans will have to address themselves when they become responsible for these islands, with their area of one hundred and fifteen thousand square miles and their semi-savage and savage population of nearly eight millions. No enterprise of like magnitude or complexity has ever lain before the United States before, for when she purchased Louisiana, and again when she conquered vast territories from Mexico, the area acquired was almost empty, and all of it was a temperate region, fit to be peopled by the overflow of her own population and to receive her institutions."

Face to face with these three problems, the American people have promptly addressed themselves to the analysis of the conditions presented, and to a tentative solution of the difficulties.

Analyzing the arguments and suggestions concerning the proper means of governing our new dependencies, we find that there are two primary questions upon which expert opinion is radically divided:

First. Does the Constitution of the United States extend of its own force to territories or dependencies governed under laws enacted by the Congress of the United States?

Second. Can white men live and thrive in the tropics?

Our views as to the proper form of government for the dependencies, or at least two of them, must be largely influenced or controlled by the answer we return to these two primary questions. If the privileges and immunities accorded to citizens of the states be the constitutional right of citizens of territories, and if the limitations placed upon Congress in legislating for states be equally effective when legislating for territories, then we must pause before attempting to govern the Porto Ricans and the Filipinos under such a system. If it be impracticable to colonize the Philippines, then our form of government, assuming we are free to fix it as we will, must differ materially from that which might be expedient in a territory suitable for colonization by Americans or kindred peoples.

Upon the first question the experts differ radically. On the one hand Professor Langdell and Professor Thayer are convinced that the constitutional limitations of the federal constitution do not apply to Congress when legislating for dependencies. The former in an article of extraordinary acuteness and logic has shown that the term "United

States" means in the constitution either (1) the collective name of the states which are united together by or under the constitution or (2) the name of the sovereign power resident in the federal union of states, and that in the latter sense it is used to express legal or political relations between the collective states and the particular states, or between the former and foreign states, or between the former and private persons, and that in this sense the term can never properly be used to express extent of territory. Only in popular usage, and not in the constitution, is the third meaning of extent of territory over which sovereignty is exercised, to be found. The three meanings may be concisely indicated by the terms Collective or United States, Federal Sovereign, Federal Empire. "The conclusion, therefore, is that, while the term 'United States' has three meanings, only the first and second of these are known to the constitution; and that is equivalent to saying that the Constitution of the United States as such does not extend beyond the limits of the states which are united by and under it." * Professor Thayer gives it as his opinion that, "there is no lack of power in our nation—of legal, constitutional power—to govern these islands as colonies, substantially as England might govern them." † On the other hand Judge Baldwin, in an article referred to by Professor Woolsey in his address opening this discussion, comes to a contrary conclusion and holds that the guaranties of the constitution extend to all territory of the United States subjected to civil government.‡ To the same effect are other recent discussions. §

Upon the second question experts also differ. It is a debatable question whether white men can live and thrive in the tropics from generation to generation. It is therefore an open question whether the Philippines will lend themselves to successful colonization. On the one hand we have the conclusion of Mr. Kidd in his suggestive essay on "The Control of the Tropics" (p. 30, see also pp. 48, 53-4) that white men cannot be acclimated in the tropics and that "the unusual triviality of the facts upon the one side, and the

* 12 Harv. Law Rev. 365 (February, 1899).
† 12 Harv. Law Rev. 464, 467 (March, 1899).
‡ 12 Harv. Law Rev. 393, 404-5 (February, 1899).
§ Carmen F. Randolph, 12 Harv. Law Rev. 291 (January, 1899); Professor J. W. Burgess, 14 Pol. Sci. Quar. 1 (March, 1899); Professor Ernst Freund, *Ib.*, 19.

apparently massive and overwhelming character of the evidence on the other, will probably bring most unbiased minds to feel that it is a matter upon which in the end there can hardly be room for any real or important difference of opinion.'' On the other hand, however, we have the testimony and the opinion of the venerable Alfred Russel Wallace (in *The Independent* for March 9, 1899, p. 667) that his observation and experience in tropical countries during a period of four years' residence in Brazil and eight in the Malay archipelago lead to the conclusion that white men can live and work and thrive in tropical lands if proper sanitary conditions are observed. Professor Blackman (*Independent*, March 9, 1899, p. 670) gives many recorded facts to sustain the same conclusion. The experience in Queensland is adduced by both Mr. Wallace and Professor Blackman to add demonstration to the theory otherwise based upon somewhat scattered and isolated facts.

Whatever the truth as to this controversy, it is well for us to take a conservative, if hopeful, view. White men are not likely to flock to the tropics as colonists until it is reasonably certain that they can live there in safety and comfort. Gold fields or diamond fields might entice them, but agriculture and manufacture give too slow a return to encourage the assumption of a large risk. It will be many years before the Philippines will be regarded as a suitable field for any extensive colonization. Moreover we must remember that the islands are already more densely populated than many of the United States and that white men rarely condescend to the harder forms of labor in the presence of large numbers of an inferior race. The Philippines, therefore, must be governed under conditions very similar to those which confront the English in India and the Dutch in Java and Sumatra.

It is, however, not the object of this paper to enlarge upon the second of these questions, or to deal with the form of government best suited to tropical dependencies; but to seek to show that whatever government may be thought best under these conditions, we are free to establish.

The solutions offered, the form of government proposed for these dependencies, is determined by each writer who has approached the problem, in accordance with his views as to the constitutional powers and limitations of Congress.

Those who believe that we are not free to govern as we please, that at every step we shall be beset by constitutional limitations wholly inapplicable to existing conditions, have two possible solutions—a military government or a protectorate. By either of these methods we should avoid all troublesome constitutional questions. By the first we should leave the power where it now resides, in the executive branch of the government. But there are two very serious objections to this. In the first place nothing seems less desirable for the American Republic than a permanent military government in any place subject to its jurisdiction. It is not only opposed to all our political notions and traditions, but it is a dangerous object lesson for a democracy. In the next place, as Professor Woolsey justly says, we should always in the case of military government, be in fear of congressional action which would plunge us into the very troubles from which military government is intended to save us. Is it not too much to hope for, even if it were well to hope for it, that Congress shall remain inactive where it has a clear right, perhaps a clear duty, to act? As a temporary expedient military government may tide us over the period of preparation, but in the near future we must squarely face the problem of settled, civil government.

A protectorate, on the other hand, means an incomplete control, limited and defined by treaty, of a people described by Professor Woolsey's citations as "incapable of gratitude, profligate, undependable, improvident, cruel, impertinent, superstitious, treacherous," a people "so averse to social order, that they can only be ruled by coercion, by the demonstration of force." Under such a treaty we should remain responsible before the world for the good conduct of the islands; we should be held to the protection of foreign interests there and should be responsible for foreign relations; we should be bound by the terms of a convention which could be changed, should experience demonstrate that change is necessary, only by the consent of the other party to it; we should, unless our first arrangement were a miracle of wisdom, be hampered more seriously than by all the provisions of the federal constitution, for that at least we can change without the consent of an Asiatic dependency.

Those who believe that we are free to govern as we please, as free as England would be under like circumstances, look forward to the establishment of a civil government suited to the needs of the dependency for which it is framed, and backed by such force as is necessary to give it stability and safety. For myself, I believe that such a government is possible and desirable. I believe that the only justifiable form of government for dependencies of the United States is a civil government adapted to the existing conditions and needs of the dependency and administered under the supervision of Congress. While giving due weight to all that may be said to the contrary, I am convinced that Congress is free to establish such a government untrammeled and unrestricted by any provisions of the federal constitution save only the prohibition against slavery. In the space now allotted to me I shall seek to show the grounds of this belief.

Let us examine the provisions of the federal constitution that may touch the matter. Bringing together all the various provisions of that instrument conferring power upon Congress and restricting the power so conferred, we find the following general scheme :

First. A specific enumeration of powers, formerly exercised by the states, but by this grant conferred upon Congress, to be exercised over territory and people formerly within the exclusive jurisdiction of the states.*

Second. A specific proviso that in the exercise of the powers so conferred, Congress shall not do certain things.†

Third. A specific statement that certain of these powers shall be exclusive and that as to these the states shall not possess concurrent powers.‡

Fourth. After all these relations between the federal power and the states are disposed of, a specific, unrestricted grant of power in these words: "The Congress shall have power to dispose of and make all needful rules and regulations respecting the territory or other property belonging to the United States."§ In this there is no hint that such power is to be limited in any way by the provisions previously inserted for the preservation of the rights and liberties of the states or of the people of the states.

* Art. I, sec. 8; Art. III.
† Art. I, sec. 9; Art. III, sec. 2, sub. 3. It is significant that the very first of these forbids Congress to prohibit for a certain period "the migration or importation of such persons as any of the *states now existing* shall think proper to admit." Of the others two specifically mention the states as the territory included in the prohibition.—Art. I, sec. 9, subs. 5 and 6.
‡ Art. I, sec. 10.
§ Art. IV, sec. 3, subs. 2.

Such are the provisions, plain and unequivocal, of the constitution as it was originally adopted. But objection was made that the limitations of Art. I, Sec. 9, and Art. III. Sec. 2, Sub. 3, did not sufficiently safeguard the states, or the people thereof, against the improper exercise of the powers conferred in Art. I, Sec. 8, and in Art. III. Thereupon the first ten amendments were adopted to meet this objection, and it is historically correct to say that these amendments have the same force and effect, and no other, as if they had originally been adopted as a part of the provisos of Art. I, Sec. 9 and Art. III.

Of the later amendments, the Fourteenth and the Fifteenth, are, with no straining of construction, but naturally and logically, to be regarded as a completion of the same purpose. The first section of the Fourteenth determines those who are citizens of the United States and of a state, and is mainly concerned in prohibiting the states from abridging the privileges of such persons. The other sections are plainly aimed at the states. The Fifteenth supplements the Fourteenth by preventing the disfranchisement of the citizens defined in the Fourteenth "on account of race, color or previous condition of servitude."

The Thirteenth Amendment, on the other hand, is by its terms, made to apply not only to the states but to any place subject to the jurisdiction of the United States. Of all the provisions of the constitution this, therefore, is the only one that in terms, or by fair implication, limits the general grant of power to govern the territories or dependencies of the United States.*

The conclusion is therefore but natural that Congress has all needful powers over the dependencies except that it cannot authorize or permit slavery to exist there.

If the question were wholly a new one, to be determined with reference to our new conditions and unembarrassed by previous pronouncements, I venture to think that this conclusion would easily be reached by the courts. But it is said that the Supreme Court has already decided adversely to this contention, and has expressed a *dictum* adverse to it

---

*With this example and purpose before them the Congress and the States adopted in the Fourteenth Amendment the phrase, "All persons born or naturalized in the United States," without a hint that it was intended to include other places subject to their jurisdiction, and the further phrase "citizens of the United States and of the state wherein they reside," without a suggestion that persons are citizens who reside outside the limits of a state. Of course the phrase "and subject to their jurisdiction" refers in this amendment to persons and not to places.

in numerous cases. After a consideration of the cases cited to these propositions, I am ready to confess that the Supreme Court has, in several cases, given utterance to *dicta* to the effect that Congress is restricted by the constitutional limitations in its dealings with the territories, and has, in one case, actually decided that the constitution guarantees to the people of the District of Columbia a trial by jury in all criminal cases. But beyond this I can find no decision of the Supreme Court to the effect claimed—and, as for the *dicta*, while they express the opinion of judges from the point of view presented in the cases in which they were uttered, we are all aware that they will not be allowed to control a subsequent decision in which the court may find it possible and proper to take a contrary view.

In order to understand the precise questions involved in these decisions and *dicta*, and to appreciate the precise questions that may arise should Congress undertake to establish a civil government for Porto Rico and the Philippines, let us arrange under appropriate heads all the restrictions upon congressional power found in the federal constitution and examine such pronouncements as have been made by the federal courts concerning them. They all fall under the following heads: (*a*) Citizenship; (*b*) Justice; (*c*) Revenue; (*d*) Bankruptcy; (*e*) Military Forces; (*f*) Titles of Nobility; (*g*) Freedom of Opinion and Speech; (*h*) Slavery.

(*a*) *Citizenship.*

1. The Congress shall have power .... to establish an uniform rule of naturalization .... throughout the United States.—Art. I, sec. 8, sub. 4.

2. All persons born or naturalized in the United States, and subject to the jurisdiction thereof, are citizens of the United States and of the state wherein they reside.—Amend. XIV, sec. 1.

3. The right of citizens of the United States to vote shall not be denied or abridged by the United States or by any state on account of race, color, or previous condition of servitude.—Amend. XV.

4. The citizens of each state shall be entitled to all privileges and immunities of citizens in the several states.—Art. IV, sec. 2, sub. 1.

Under this head the first provision and the last may be passed over. I am sure there will be a general agreement that the last is by its terms a restriction upon the states and not upon the United States, and that as applied to the states it comprehends only those privileges and immunities which are in their nature fundamental, as protection by the government, the enjoyment of life and liberty with the right to acquire and enjoy property subject to such restraints as the government may justly prescribe for the public good.* It is now too plain for argument that when the word state is used in the constitution it refers to one of the members of the Union and does not include the District of Columbia or the territories.† Internationally it may be otherwise, and the word state in a treaty may include any political entity whose foreign affairs are conducted by the federal government.‡ This distinction between the meaning of phrases as used in the constitution and the same phrases as used in international law is very important, though it has sometimes been overlooked by commentators.

As to the first of the above provisions, it is proper to make two observations: First, I cannot conceive that we should be at all embarrassed by allowing the same persons to be naturalized in Porto Rico or the Philippines as in Florida or California; second, the remarks which follow as to the second and third provisions above quoted and to the rule requiring taxes to be uniform throughout the United States, are equally applicable to this provision, and, if justified, establish that the phrase United States means the states united by and under the constitution.

The second and third provisions—the Fourteenth and Fifteenth Amendments—present a question of the very first importance. Will all persons hereafter born in Porto Rico or the Philippines or Hawaii be citizens of the United States under the definition contained in the Fourteenth Amendment and entitled to the protection of that and the Fifteenth Amendment? I wish to point out that the answer to this question is not dependent, in my judgment, upon the establishment of a civil government in these islands. Under whose jurisdiction are the Porto Ricans and the Filipinos and the Hawaiians? Not Spain's, for hers has been yielded to the United States. Not that of a Porto Rican or Filipino or Hawaiian government for there is none *de jure* or *de facto*. It cannot be that any one of these groups is derelict and without a government to exercise jurisdiction. There remains but one answer. From the moment the treaty of cession is in effect the islands and the inhabitants thereof are

* Corfield *v.* Coryell, 4 Wash. C. C. 371; McCready *v.* Virginia, 94 U. S. 391; Geer *v.* Connecticut, 161 U. S. 519.

† Hepburn *v.* Ellzey, 2 Cranch, 445; New Orleans *v.* Winter, 1 Wheaton, 91; Barney *v.* Baltimore, 6 Wallace, 280.

‡ Geofroy *v.* Riggs, 133 U. S. 258.

subject to the jurisdiction of the United States, and if the islands are a part of the United States, within the meaning of the Fourteenth and Fifteenth Amendments, then every child born in them after the treaty is effective, is a citizen of the United States with all a citizen's privileges and immunities, and the United States cannot deny to such citizen the right to vote on account of race or color. While those provisions of the constitution which are expressly or impliedly an inhibition upon Congress could not be operative in any event, until Congress chose to act, this provision, which simply defines citizenship, does not wait upon any act of Congress, any more than does the provision of the Thirteenth Amendment. The sole question is, whether, like the Thirteenth Amendment, it is operative in all places subject to the jurisdiction of the United States.

But are persons born in these islands born in the United States within the meaning of the constitution? The answer to this question must depend upon the meaning given to the term "United States." If the contention of Professor Langdell is correct—and I believe that it is—then the term must be taken, for constitutional and legal purpose, in its natural, primary meaning of the states united or federated under the constitution. A person born in one of these is a citizen of the United States (the federal sovereign), and of the state where he resides; no state shall make any law to abridge his privileges or immunities as such citizen; neither the state nor the United States shall deny to him the suffrage on account of race, color or previous condition of servitude. But the status of a person born outside the limits of the states so united or federated is not defined by the constitution made and established for such states, but by the law of nations, the common law, and such statutes as may be enacted by Congress, precisely as the status of persons born in the states was thus defined before these amendments went into effect. Here we come again to the distinction between the constitutional and the international definition or use of terms. A state in the constitution means one of the United States; in international law it means any political entity over which the United States, in external affairs, exercises jurisdiction. A citizen in the constitution means a person born or naturalized in one of the United States and subject to their jurisdiction; it means in international law a person born in any place subject to the jurisdiction of the United States and himself subject to such jurisdiction. That this is the natural meaning to be attached to the term as defined in the constitution will be apparent upon a little consideration. When we reflect that these amendments were aimed at states lately in rebellion, that the restrictions contained in them are mainly in terms restrictions upon the states, that there is a specific statement that the person shall be a citizen "of the United States and of the state," that with the example of the Thirteenth Amendment before them Congress and the states would have used a more comprehensive phrase had they intended to include the territories or other places subject to the jurisdiction of the United States that, finally, there is no reason here or elsewhere, save in the Thirteenth Amendment, to impute any intention to extend the constitutional limitations beyond the states framing the constitution, but, on the contrary, there is every reason to suppose that such limitations are imposed for the protection of the states and the people thereof, we are bound, it seems to me, to conclude that, while persons born in the dependencies may be citizens of the United States in the international sense or the sense known to the common law, or may be made citizens for specified purposes by statute or treaty, they are not such by force of any constitutional provision and are subject, therefore, in all internal relations, to such laws as Congress in its wisdom may see fit to enact.

I am not unaware that there are *dicta*—particularly in the *Slaughter-House Cases**—which make against this conclusion. But it need hardly be said that *dicta* uttered by a judge twenty-five years ago in deciding whether an act of the State of Louisiana which created a monopoly in the business of running a slaughter-house was constitutional, would have very little weight before the same court when called upon to decide the constitutional status of the inhabitants of the Philippine Archipelago. It has, indeed, been decided that a person, though of Asiatic parentage, born in one of the states, is a citizen of the United States and of the state.† But it has never been decided that a person born in a territory is a citizen of the United States within the meaning of these amendments, while it has been decided that an Indian born a member of an Indian tribe is not a

---

* 16 Wallace, 36
† United States *v* Wong Kim Ark, 169 U. S. 649.

citizen of the United States although he voluntarily separates himself from his tribe and takes up his residence among the white citizens of a state.*

It is probably competent for Congress to enlarge, though not to restrict, the definition of citizenship found in the Fourteenth Amendment. Congress may, therefore, by suitable legislation determine what inhabitants of territories or what Indians born in tribal relations shall be deemed citizens.† It is also competent for the treaty-making power in acquiring territory to establish by treaty the status as to citizenship of the inhabitants of the territory. This was in fact done in all treaties of cession prior to the one ceding Porto Rico and the Philippines.‡ But such citizenship, whether established by statute or treaty, is a legislative and not a constitutional citizenship. What the treaty-making power or the legislative power may grant it may withhold. As the treaty ceding Porto Rico and the Philippines is silent on this point, it therefore rests with Congress to grant or withhold citizenship for internal purposes to the inhabitants of those dependencies. It is unnecessary now to inquire whether, if once granted, such grant may afterwards be withdrawn.

(b) Justice.

1. The judicial power of the United States shall be vested in one Supreme Court, and in such inferior courts as the Congress may from time to time ordain and establish. The judges, both of the supreme and inferior courts, shall hold their offices during good behavior, and shall, at stated times, receive for their services a compensation, which shall not be diminished during their continuance in office. The judicial power shall extend to all cases in law and equity, arising under this constitution, the laws of the United States, and treaties made, or which shall be made, under their authority, ... to all cases of admiralty and maritime jurisdiction, etc.—Art. III, secs. 1 and 2.

2. The trial of all crimes, except in cases of impeachment, shall be by jury; and such trial shall be held in the state where the said crimes shall have been committed; but when not committed within any state, the trial shall be at such place or places as the Congress may by law have directed.—Art. III, sec. 2, sub. 3.

*Elk v. Wilkins, 112 U. S., 94.

†Indian Land-in-Severalty Act of February 8, 1887 Sec. 6, found in 24 Statutes-at-Large, p. 388.

‡Art. III of the treaty of cession of Louisiana ; Art. VI of treaty of cession of Florida ; Art. IX of treaty of 1848, and Art. V of treaty of 1853, with Mexico ; Art. III of treaty of cession of Alaska. Referring to the treaty of cession of Florida, Chief Justice Marshall in American Ins. Co. v. Canter (1 Peters 511, 542), says: " This treaty is the law of the land and admits the inhabitants of Florida to the enjoyment of the privileges and immunities of the citizens of the United States."

3. No person shall be held to answer for a capital or otherwise infamous crime, unless on a presentment or indictment of a grand jury, except in cases arising in the land or naval forces, or in the militia, when in actual service in time of war or public danger; nor shall any person be subject for the same offence to be twice put in jeopardy of life or limb; nor shall be compelled in any criminal case to be a witness against himself, nor be deprived of life, liberty or property, without due process of law; nor shall private property be taken for public use without just compensation.—Amend. V.

4. In all criminal prosecutions the accused shall enjoy the right to a speedy and public trial, by an impartial jury of the state and district wherein the crime shall have been committed, which district shall have been previously ascertained by law, and to be informed of the nature and cause of the accusation; to be confronted with the witnesses against him; to have compulsory process for obtaining witnesses in his favor, and to have the assistance of counsel for his defence.—Amend. VI.

5. In suits at common law, where the value in controversy shall exceed twenty dollars, the right of trial by jury shall be preserved, and no fact tried by a jury shall be otherwise re-examined in any court of the United States, than according to the rules of the common law. —Amend. VII.

6. Excessive bail shall not be required, nor excessive fines imposed, nor cruel and unusual punishments inflicted.—Amend. VIII.

7. The privilege of the writ of *habeas corpus* shall not be suspended, unless when in cases of rebellion or invasion the public safety may require it.—Art. I, sec. 9, subs. 2.

8. No bill of attainder or *ex post facto* law shall be passed.—Art. I, sec. 9, sub. 3.

9. The right of the people to be secure in their persons, houses, papers, and effects, against unreasonable searches and seizures, shall not be violated, and no warrants shall issue, but upon probable cause, supported by oath or affirmation, and particularly describing the place to be searched, and the persons or things to be seized.—Amend. IV.

These provisions govern the power of Congress in the establishment of courts and in the enactment of laws for the administration of justice in the courts so established.

Among the earliest decisions as to the powers of Congress over the territories were those concerning the establishment of courts, and it was distinctly held that these powers are plenary and are unrestricted by the provisions of Article III, Section 1. At the outset of our inquiries into the meaning of the provisions concerning the administration of justice, we find that under the decisions of the Supreme Court, the first provision quoted above, has no reference whatever to the territories, that Congress may establish there such courts as it sees fit, give to them such jurisdiction as it pleases, provide for the appointment of judges whose terms of office shall be limited and subject them to removal from office at the pleasure of the appointing power.* The leading case on this is the case of the American Insurance Company v. Canter (1 Peters, 511), in which, in the course of his argument, Webster, one of the counsel in the case, used this significant language:

"What is Florida? It is no part of the United States. How can it be? How is it represented? Do the laws of the United States reach Florida? Not unless by particular provisions. The territory and all within it are to be governed by the acquiring power, except where there are reservations by treaty. By the law of England, when possession is taken of territories, the king, *Jure Coronae*, has the power of legislation until parliament shall interfere. Congress have the *Jus Coronae* in this case, and Florida was to be governed by Congress as she thought proper. What has Congress done? She might have done anything; she might have refused the trial by jury, and refused a legislature. She has given a legislature to be exercised at her will; and a government of a mixed nature, in which she has endeavored to distinguish between state and the United States jurisdiction, anticipating the future erection of the territory into a state. Does the law establishing the court at Key West come within the restrictions of the Constitution of the United States? If the constitution does not extend over this territory, the law cannot be inconsistent with the national constitution."

Chief Justice Marshall, in his opinion in the case, does not go to this length, but he decides for the court in favor of the power of Congress to establish such courts as it pleases in the territories, either directly or through the territorial legislature, and to confer upon them such jurisdiction as it thinks proper. He says:

"These courts, then, are not constitutional courts, in which the judicial power conferred by the constitution on the general government, can be deposited. They are incapable of receiving it. They are legislative courts, created in virtue of the general right of sovereignty which exists in the government, or in virtue of that clause which enables Congress to make all needful rules and regulations, respecting the territory belonging to the United States. The jurisdiction with which they are invested is not a part of that judicial power which is defined in the third article of the constitution, but is conferred by Congress, in the execution of those general powers which that body possesses over the territories of the United States. Although admiralty jurisdiction can be exercised in the states in those courts only, which are established in pursuance of the third article of the constitution, the same limitation does not extend to the territories. In legislating for them, Congress exercises the combined powers of the general, and of a state government."

* Serè v. Pilot, 6 Cranch, 332; American Insurance Company v. Canter, 1 Peters, 511; Benner v. Porter, 9 Howard, 235; Clinton v. Englebrecht, 13 Wallace, 434; Reynolds v. United States, 98 U. S. 145; The City of Panama, 101 U. S. 453; McAllister v. United States, 141 U. S. 174.

In Clinton *v.* Englebrecht (13 Wallace, 434), Chief Justice Chase reiterates the same doctrine, in these words:

"There is no Supreme Court of the United States, nor is there any District Court of the United States, in the sense of the constitution, in the territory of Utah. The judges are not appointed for the same terms, nor is the jurisdiction which they exercise part of the judicial power conferred by the constitution or the general government. The courts are the legislative courts of the territories, created in virtue of the clause which authorizes Congress to make all needful rules and regulations respecting the territories belonging to the United States."

It is clear then that "the judicial power of the United States" means the judicial power of the federal government as exercised within the territory comprising the states, and has no reference to the judicial powers exercised in the territories.

As to the provisions guaranteeing trial by jury, the first is found in Article III, immediately following the provision for the establishment of courts and defining their jurisdiction, and is plainly intended to fix the procedure and safeguards in the courts so established. We have just seen that that provision for the establishment of courts does not apply to the territories, but that the territorial courts are established under the general unrestricted grant of power "to make all needful rules and regulations respecting the territory . . . belonging to the United States." Since therefore the territorial courts do not owe their existence to Article III, is it logical or reasonable to hold that they are restricted by the provisions of Article III? Since they do owe their existence to the broad legislative grant in Article IV, is it not necessary to conclude that they are restricted in their powers and procedure by the legislation creating them and by that alone? In other words all constitutional courts—that is, the Supreme Court and the inferior courts created in the United States—are subject to constitutional limitations, but the legislative courts—that is, the territorial courts—are not subject to constitutional but to legislative limitations.

The provisions in Amendments V, VI and VII, are, historically, to be read as if a part of Article III, and to be construed in the same manner as the provisions just considered. The same is true of the other provisions dealing with judicial writs, procedure and punishment. All of them except two are found in the first ten amendments, and those two are in Article I, Section 9 (sub-sections 2 and 3) which, as we have seen, limits logically the powers of Congress conferred in Article I, Section 8, in legislating for the territory or the people of the states united under the constitution.

There is one decision and there are some *dicta* that stand in the way of so construing these provisions—especially as to the right to trial by jury. The decision is in Callan *v.* Wilson (127 U. S. 540), where the Supreme Court holds that a citizen of the District of Columbia has a constitutional right to a trial by jury when charged with a crime, and that an act of Congress denying this right is unconstitutional. Upon this case, which must be distinguished or overruled if the construction here contended for is to be established, these observations are proper. First, the grant of legislative power "over such district as may, by cession of particular states and the acceptance of Congress, become the seat of government of the United States," is contained in Article I, Section 8, along with the other grants of power conferred by the states and is followed by and may perhaps be regarded as limited by, the same restrictions as the other grants. Second, the grant contemplates the transfer of territory and people then governed by some state to the United States, and it is not unreasonable to think that the states were desirous of securing for this territory and people the same protection as for the states themselves; finally, as observed by Professor Langdell in another connection, "the constitution once extended over it, and it may not be easy to show that it has ever ceased to extend over it.*

In the case of the American Publishing Co. *v.* Fisher (166 U. S. 464), where an act of the Territory of Utah which provided that "in civil cases a verdict may be rendered on the concurrence of nine or more members of the jury," was held invalid as contravening the act under which Utah was admitted as a territory, the court leaves undecided the question whether the Seventh Amendment applies. The state of the decisions on this point is thus concisely summarized by Mr. Justice Brewer:

"Whether the Seventh Amendment to the Constitution of the United States, which provides that 'in suits at common law, where the value in controversy shall exceed twenty dollars, the right of trial by jury shall be preserved,' operates *ex proprio vigore* to invalidate

---

* 12 Harv. Law Rev., p. 382.

this statute, may be a matter of dispute. In Webster *v.* Reid, 11 How. 437, an act of the legislature of the Territory of Iowa dispensing with a jury in a certain class of common law actions was held void. While in the opinion, on page 460, the Seventh Amendment was quoted, it was also said: 'The organic law of the Territory of Iowa, by express provision and by reference, extended the laws of the United States, including the ordinance of 1787, over the territory, so far as they are applicable;' and the ordinance of 1787, article 2, in terms provided that 'the inhabitants of the said territory shall always be entitled to the benefits of the writ of *habeas corpus,* and of the trial by jury." So the invalidity may have been adjudged by reason of the conflict with congressional legislation. In Reynolds *v.* United States, 98 U. S. 145, 154, it was said, in reference to a criminal case coming from the Territory of Utah, that 'by the Constitution of the United States (Amendment VI) the accused was entitled to a trial by an impartial jury.' Both of these cases were quoted in Callan *v.* Wilson, 127 U. S. 540, as authorities to sustain the ruling that the provisions in the Constitution of the United States relating to trial by jury are in force in the District of Columbia. On the other hand, in Mormon Church *v.* United States, 136 U. S. 1, 44, it was said by Mr. Justice Bradley, speaking for the court: 'Doubtless Congress in legislating for the territories would be subject to those fundamental limitations in favor of personal rights which are formulated in the constitution and its amendments; but these limitations would exist rather by inference and the general spirit of the constitution from which Congress derives all its powers, than by any express and direct application of its provisions.' And in McAllister *v.* United States, 141 U. S. 174, it was held that the constitutional provision in respect to the tenure of judicial offices did not apply to territorial judges."

In the case of Springville *v.* Thomas (166 U. S. 707), involving the same question, broader language is used by Chief Justice Fuller, but the decision is sufficiently rested upon the ground stated in American Publishing Co. *v.* Fisher.

In the later case of Thompson *v.* Utah (170 U. S. 343), it was decided that the provision of the constitution of the State of Utah that in criminal cases, other than capital, the jury should consist of eight jurors, was unconstitutional as to crimes committed prior to the adoption of the state constitution, as contravening the provision of Article I, Section 10, Sub. 1, of the federal constitution prohibiting any state from passing an *ex post facto* law. But the court went further and argued that the provisions of the national constitution relating to trials by jury apply to the territories. That this was extra judicial may be seen from the following considerations: (1) the law of the territory (independent of the Constitution of the United States) provided that a trial jury should consist of twelve persons; (2) the crime was committed while the law was in effect; (3) subsequently the state constitution provided for the trial of this crime by a jury of eight persons; (4) therefore this provision of the state constitution was *ex post facto* as to this crime. In all this there is no question of Article III, Section 2, or of the Sixth Amendment, but only of Article I, Section 10, Sub. 1, which prohibits a state from passing an *ex post facto* law. That this is the understanding of the reporter is evident from the head note of the case which simply states, as the holding of the court that, "the provision in the constitution of the State of Utah, providing for the trial of criminal cases, not capital, in courts of general jurisdiction by a jury composed of eight persons, is *ex post facto* in its application to felonies committed before the territory became a state." Precisely the same decision would be necessary had the first act been passed after Utah was a state, the crime committed while the act was in force, and then the provision of the constitution had altered the prior act by substituting a jury of eight persons for a jury of twelve. The argument, therefore, that the right of the accused rested upon the provisions of the federal constitution guaranteeing trial by jury, was wholly unnecessary to the decision of the case.*

We may set over against the decision in Callan *v.* Wilson and the *dicta* in the other cases the decision in *In re* Ross (140 U. S. 453), where it was held that a consular court established by Congress in Japan, and consisting of a consul and four associates, could try, convict and sentence to death an American citizen without any jury at all. This is rested upon the ground that the constitution cannot have any effect outside of the territory of the United States and that, therefore, the accused is not within the protection of the provisions relating to jury trial. Such is the contention of this paper. The constitution cannot have any effect outside the states united by and under it, unless by express terms (as in the Thirteenth Amendment) it is extended to places "subject to their jurisdiction." It is, of course, clear that the territory of Japan is not within the United States in any sense. What is here contended for is that the territories, lying outside the limits of the states, are not within the

* As much so as the argument of the judges in Dred Scott *v.* Sanford (19 Howard, 393), that Congress had not power to prohibit slavery in the territories.

United States, in the sense in which that term is used in the constitution, although they are within the United States in the international and popular sense of the term.

Further light may be had from the consideration of the sovereignty of the United States over the Indian tribes. In the government of them the federal power has never regarded itself as circumscribed or limited by the provisions of the constitution. It is true the policy for a long time was to govern them through treaties, but this policy has lately been abandoned and they are now largely governed under legislation of Congress. The powers of Congress in this matter were considered in United States v. Kagama (118 U. S. 375), and it was there held that an act defining crimes committed by one Indian against another upon an Indian reservation, situated in a state, and conferring jurisdiction over such crimes upon the federal courts, was a constitutional exercise of congressional power, and that the state had no jurisdiction over Indians as long as they maintain their tribal relations. "These Indian tribes," it is said, "are the wards of the nation. They are communities *dependent* upon the United States." Therefore the United States has exclusive jurisdiction over them, as it has over the territories, and there is, it seems, no constitutional restriction upon the exercise of this jurisdiction.

Congress may therefore establish such courts and provide such procedure as it deems expedient in foreign territory or for Indian tribes, and is not restricted by any provisions of the federal constitution. If the reasoning of this paper be sound, it may in like manner establish such courts and provide such procedure as it deems expedient in any territory not subject to the jurisdiction of a state of the Union. To quote the language of Mr. Justice Brown in the recent case of Holden v. Hardy (169 U. S. 366, 389):

"In the future growth of the nation, as heretofore, it is not impossible that Congress may see fit to annex territories whose jurisprudence is that of the civil law. One of the considerations moving to such annexation might be the very fact that the territory so annexed should enter the Union with its traditions, laws and systems of administration unchanged. It would be a narrow construction of the constitution to require them to abandon these, or to substitute for a system, which represented the growth of generations of inhabitants, a jurisprudence with which they had no previous acquaintance or sympathy."

This statement, although made in another connection, and in the course of a determination of the powers of a state, is nevertheless significant as indicative of an attitude of mind which would make it possible for the Supreme Court to give effect, under the constitution, to legislation of Congress adapted to dependencies whose jurisprudence is certainly not that of the common law however close or remote may be its relation to the civil law.

(c) *Revenue.*

1. The Congress shall have power to lay and collect taxes, duties, imposts and excises . . .; but all duties, imposts and excises shall be uniform throughout the United States.—Art. I, Sec. 8, Subs. 1.

2. No capitation or other direct tax shall be laid, unless in proportion to the census or enumeration hereinbefore directed to be taken.—Art. I, Sec. 9, Subs. 4.

3. No tax or duty shall be laid on articles exported from any state. —Art. I, Sec. 9, Subs. 5.

4. No preference shall be given by any regulation of commerce or revenue to the ports of one state over those of another; nor shall vessels bound to, or from, one state, be obliged to enter, clear, or pay duties in another.—Art. I, Sec. 9, Subs. 6

Under the provisions as to means of raising revenue, it may be observed that only the first provision (Art. I, Sec. 8, Subs. 1) could possibly present any difficulty to Congress in the governing of dependencies. As to this, what has already been said concerning citizenship applies here *mutatis mutandis*. The restriction as to uniformity of duties, imposts and excises throughout the United States would be very embarrassing, if it should be held applicable to territory lying outside the limits of any state. But there is no good reason for thinking that it is applicable to such territory, while many reasons may be assigned for holding the contrary. First it is found in the very first grant of power to Congress by the states, and is clearly intended to restrict Congress in exercising the powers yielded by the states over their own territory and people. Second, the term "United States" as here used clearly means the states uniting in the formation of this instrument and those that should thereafter be admitted upon the same terms. Third, the subsequent grant of full powers over the territory belonging to the federal sovereign contains no hint that these prior restrictions are intended to limit or restrict that power.

There is, indeed, a *dictum* in an early case that makes against this construction. In Loughborough *v.* Blake

(5 Wheaton, 317), decided in 1820, Chief Justice Marshall was called upon to decide whether an act of Congress including the District of Columbia in an apportionment of a direct annual tax of $6,000,000 previously laid upon the states, was constitutional. The decision could be rested squarely upon the grant of full legislative power over the District found in Article I, Section 8, subsection 17, but the chief justice indulges in some extra judicial observations as to the meaning of the term "United States" as used in Article I, Section 8, Subsection 1, in the course of which he lays it down that the term includes the states and territories. Yet in the later case of American Insurance Company v. Canter (1 Peters, 511) he rests the decision upon the general grant of powers over the territories as distinguished from the states, while Webster in his argument flatly denies that the restrictions applicable to legislative power over the states have any force in the exercise of legislative power over the territories, and neither the court nor the counsel make any reference to the *dictum* in this case. The case, moreover, has never since been cited by the court as sustaining the view taken by the chief justice. Even if we were to give weight to the *dictum*, we could still distinguish the case on the same ground as the case of Callan v. Wilson (*Ante*, p. 34), namely, that it is concerned, not with the grant of power over the territories, found in Article IV, but with the special grant of power over the district ceded for the seat of government, found in Article I, Section 8. That this is the correct view seems to be confirmed by the explanation given of Loughborough v. Blake in Gibbons v. District of Columbia (116 U. S. 404, 407).

The case of Cross v. Harrison (16 Howard, 164) is also sometimes cited as teaching a doctrine contrary to the position here taken. But that case simply decided that, after the treaty of cession of California by Mexico, and before Congress had legislated concerning the territory, the Executive Department might lawfully collect an import duty at San Francisco as at other ports of the United States. This is rested upon the argument that, in the absence of a contrary provision in the treaty, the territory became instantly bound and privileged by the laws Congress had previously passed to raise a revenue on imports and tonnage. Even conceding that this is sound reasoning, it is very far from saying that Congress could not, or the treaty-making power could not, have provided a different system for the territory. A statement that acts of Congress which, when passed, covered states and territories, would extend of their own force to after-acquired territory, unless differently stipulated in the treaty of cession, is no support whatever for the proposition that the constitution will extend of its own force to such territory. It seems to me that the case carries a distinct recognition of the right of the treaty-making power or of Congress to provide a different system for the territory, and that the decision is rested upon the omission in the treaty to provide for any different system. I think it proper to add, further, that in my judgment the case could be sufficiently rested upon the power of the Executive to administer the territory in the absence of legislation, and that in such administration the Executive might, in his discretion, though he would not be bound so to do, adopt the existing tariff rates of the rest of the country. But however this may be, there is certainly nothing in this case that upholds the contention that Congress is constitutionally bound to provide import duties in the territories uniform with those in the states.

(*d*) *Bankruptcy Acts.*
The Congress shall have power . . . to establish . . . *uniform* laws on the subject of bankruptcies throughout the United States.—Art. I, Sec. 8, Subs. 4.

This provision is to be construed in the same manner as the provision as to uniform revenue laws or uniform naturalization laws. It occurs in the same subsection as the latter, and all that has been said on the other two provisions as to "uniform" laws is applicable to this provision. In any event the provision could hardly be a source of embarrassment in legislating for the dependencies.

(*e*) *Military Forces.*
1. A well-regulated militia, being necessary to the security of a free state, the right of the people to keep and bear arms, shall not be infringed.—Amend. II.
2. No soldier shall, in time of peace, be quartered in any house without the consent of the owner, nor in time of war, but in a manner to be prescribed by law.—Amend. III.

The first of these provisions contains a clear intimation that it is intended for the security of the states. A territory is not a "free state;" it is a dependency to be governed as Congress may deem expedient. As it is thus within the power of Congress, there would be an absurdity in holding that it is to be given a right to bear arms in order to resist the exercise of that power. A territorial militia may be authorized or not by Congress, just as a state militia may be authorized or not by a state. While, therefore, some have urged that this provision would entitle the Porto Ricans or the Filipinos to bear arms, and thus prepare for insurrections, it seems almost too clear for argument that no such construction could properly be put upon the provision, even if the contention as to the whole of these amendments, namely, that they are intended only for the protection of states, should be inadmissible.

The second provision could be no source of embarrassment. But, of course, like all the others, it must, on the theory here advanced, be held to be no restriction upon the powers of Congress in dealing with the territories.

(*f*) *Titles of Nobility.*

No title of nobility shall be granted by the United States.—Art. I, Sec. 9, Subs. 8.

In its terms this is the broadest of all the provisions found in the constitution as originally passed. While the construction contended for in this paper should, of course, extend to this provision also, it could be of no consequence practically whether it were so construed or not. It is very doubtful whether any circumstances could ever arise calling for a construction of it.

(*g*) *Freedom of Opinion and Speech.*

Congress shall make no law respecting an establishment of religion, or prohibiting the free exercise thereof; or abridging the freedom of speech, or of the press; or the right of the people peaceably to assemble, and to petition the government for a redress of grievances.—Amend. I.

Of all the amendments this is the broadest in its terms. But it should have no different construction than any of the other of the first ten amendments. Each is intended to secure to the states or the people thereof, an immunity against the aggressions of the federal power. Even if, however, it should be held to protect equally the people of a dependency, it is difficult to see how it would interfere with the proper government of such dependency, as it is altogether improbable that Congress would think it expedient to exercise any one of the powers prohibited in the amendment.

(*h*) *Slavery.*

Neither slavery nor involuntary servitude, except as a punishment for crime whereof the party shall have been duly convicted, shall exist within the United States, or any place subject to their jurisdiction.—Amend. XIII.

This provision is the only one found in the constitution which in terms limits the powers of Congress in dealing with the territories. The latter are subject to the jurisdiction of the United States, and therefore within the protection of the amendment prohibiting slavery. It is a very significant fact, throwing light upon the view of Congress and the states as to the meaning of the other constitutional limitations that the phrase, "or any place subject to their jurisdiction," should have been inserted in this amendment. If, as has been urged by some, all the limitations extend to the states and territories alike, that is to all places subject to the jurisdiction of the United States, why should Congress and the states have been anxious to insert here a phrase expressly including the territories? If the phrases, "throughout the United States," "within the United States," used elsewhere in the constitution, mean throughout or within all territory over which the federal sovereign has jurisdiction, then the phrase here used is not only useless, but dangerous, for while it adds nothing, it throws a grave doubt at once upon the meaning of the phrases previously used. Is it not obvious that it was inserted because the other phrases were understood to mean throughout or within the territory of the states united under the constitution, while as to this amendment the Congress and the states meant to go further and include that territory and also the territory over which by Article I, Section 8, subsection 17, and Article IV, Section 3, subsection 2, Congress has been given plenary power?

These are all the provisions of the constitution that restrict the powers of Congress. These are all the important decisions of the Supreme Court, save one, that directly consider the question whether Congress is subject to any of these restrictions, or to any restrictions, in legislating for the territories. It still remains to consider the case of Dred Scott *v.* Sanford (19 Howard, 393). Scott claimed his freedom on two grounds: that he had been taken by his master to the free state of Illinois and had resided there two years; that he had then been taken to the free territory of Upper Louisiana (now Minnesota) where slavery was prohibited under an act of Congress ('The Missouri Compromise), and had resided there two years. He had then been taken back to the State of Missouri where he had since resided and where he now sued for his freedom. The question on its merits was whether residence in the free state or the free territory, followed by a return to the slave state, worked an emancipation. The decision on the merits was simply this: residence in a free state or a free territory followed by a return to and residence in a slave state will have such effect, and no other, as the latter state may by the decisions of its highest court give to it; the highest court of Missouri gave no extra-territorial effect to the laws prohibiting slavery in the state and territory in which Scott had resided and deemed him on his return to Missouri still a slave; therefore the federal court was bound to follow the same holding. This disposed of the case on its merits, without any inquiry into the validity or constitutionality of the law prohibiting slavery in the territory, for admitting it to be valid and constitutional it could have no larger effect in working the emancipation of Scott than the confessedly valid law of Illinois. But a majority of the court went further and in opinions clearly extra-judicial held the act of Congress prohibiting slavery in the territory to be unconstitutional. This is put on the singularly narrow ground that the ample grant of power to Congress "to make all needful rules and regulations respecting the territory or other property belonging to the United States" is confined to territory belonging to the United States at the time the constitution was adopted "and cannot, by any just rule of interpretation, be extended to territory which the new government might afterwards obtain from a foreign nation." The sole right to acquire such territory is found in the provision for the admission of new states. Upon this is built up a novel doctrine as to the limited powers which Congress, as the agent or trustee of the states, may temporarily exercise in governing a territory so acquired while nursing it toward statehood, a doctrine now laid up among the discredited curiosities of the law together with all the rest of the extra-judicial utterances of this celebrated case. I suppose no one would now seriously cite the Dred Scott decision as authority for the proposition that Congress has not full power to govern the territories as it may deem most expedient. Certainly that the main premise of the Dred Scott argument is unsound and discredited is shown by the statement in Utter *v.* Franklin (172 U. S. 416, 423) that, "this court has repeatedly held that Congress has full legislative power over the territories, as full as that which a state legislature has over its municipal corporations."

Aside from the Dred Scott case and the others previously cited, the pronouncements of the Supreme Court upon the question of constitutional limitations upon the power defined in Utter *v.* Franklin have been in terms indicative of a vague constitutional theory rather than of a settled constitutional doctrine. Such is the statement of Mr. Justice Matthews in Murphy *v.* Ramsey (114 U. S. 15, 44) that, "the personal and civil rights of the inhabitants of the territories are secured to them, as to other citizens, by the principles of constitutional liberty which restrain all the agencies of government, state or national." Such, also, is the statement of Mr. Justice Bradley in Mormon Church *v.* United States (136 U. S. 1, 44-5), repeated by Mr. Justice Harlan in McAllister *v.* United States (141 U. S. 174, 188), that, "doubtless Congress in legislating for the territories would be subject to those fundamental limitations in favor of personal rights which are formulated in the constitution and its amendments; but these limitations would exist rather by inference and the general spirit of the constitution, from which Congress derives all its powers, than by any express and direct applications of its provisions."

We need hardly dwell upon such pronouncement. We may rather recur to the classic statement of Chief Justice Marshall in Cohens *v.* Virginia (6 Wheaton, 264, 399): "It is a maxim not to be disregarded that general expressions, in every opinion, are to be taken in connection with the case in which those expressions are used. If they go beyond the case, they may be respected, but ought not to control the judgment in a subsequent suit when the very point is presented for decision. The reason of this maxim is obvious. The question actually before the court is investigated with care, and considered in its full extent. Other principles which may serve to illustrate it, are considered in their relation to the case decided, but their possible bearing on all other cases is seldom completely investigated." This maxim we may now invoke. New conditions never contemplated by the judges who voiced these general expressions have suddenly arisen. Those expressions may be respected as applicable to the cases in which they were used, but they will hardly control the judgment of the judges who shall be called upon to decide the weighty questions involved in the government of remote island dependencies.

When those questions arise for settlement it will be possible to hold, with entire loyalty to the constitution, and respect for judicial decisions, that all dependencies, except the District of Columbia, are governed under the general power given to Congress "to dispose of and make all needful rules and regulations respecting the territory or other property belonging to the United States;" that this power is limited only by the provision prohibiting slavery within the United States or any place subject to their jurisdiction; that no decision of the Supreme Court holds that any other limit is placed upon the powers of Congress over the territories; and that such *dicta* as may be found to the contrary are either wholly discredited or resolve themselves into a mere statement of constitutional or political theory.

THE GOVERNMENT OF DEPENDENCIES.

A. LAWRENCE LOWELL, ESQ., *Harvard University.*

One whose knowledge of our new possessions is derived entirely from books must speak upon the problem of their government with diffidence. The only thing of which he can be absolutely sure is the defectiveness of his own information, its insufficiency as a basis for conclusive inductions, and all that he can do is to offer suggestions derived from the experience of other countries under conditions that have at least a considerable similarity with those we are called upon to face. Our policy must at first be tentative, and no doubt we shall make mistakes; but we certainly want to approach the problem with such light as can be drawn from the successes and failures of other nations, and all that the writer ventures to hope is that the few suggestions that can be offered in a paper of this length will contribute something toward setting forth the questions which our government must solve.

In this discussion I shall make two assumptions. First, that our primary aim is to be the welfare of the dependencies. Such an attitude is alone worthy of an enlightened nation, and the history of colonization shows that it is almost, if not quite, impossible to make colonies a permanent benefit to the dominant country on any other basis. The dependencies ought eventually to be self-supporting, but we have no right to expect them to be a source of public revenue. The second assumption is that the provisions of the Constitution of the United States do not apply to our new possessions in such a way as to interfere seriously with the establishment of the most desirable form of administration. This assumption is, I believe, well founded, but the subject is a large one, and cannot be treated in the space to which this paper must necessarily be confined.

Within a year we have acquired three groups of islands, all within the tropic of Cancer, but differing from one another radically in the character of their people and in the nature of the problems they present. In one of them, Hawaii, there is a considerable element of Anglo-Saxon origin, which is, indeed, small as compared with the total population, but is to-day, and is apparently destined to remain, the ruling class in the island. It is not improbable, therefore, that our institutions can be immediately applied to the Sandwich Islands without modification, and such is the recommendation of the commissioners appointed to consider the subject. They have reported, in effect, in favor of a territorial government copied from the pattern that has proved successful in the West.

The other annexations present problems which are not only more difficult, but are as unlike each other as either of them is to that of Hawaii. There is, in fact, a vital difference between Porto Rico and the Philippines. Civilization in Porto Rico, as in the United States, is essentially European, and hence our aim must be to develop the people in the lines of our own life. Their condition is not so far from ours, and their climate is not so far tropical, as to set up an impassable barrier; and if it is possible to bring them into accord with our political, social and economic standards, every consideration of their welfare and our own should lead us to do so.

In the Philippines, on the other hand, which are strictly tropical in climate, the civilization, like that of India, of the Malay Peninsula and of Borneo, is mainly indigenous, and hence we ought to endeavor, as the English have done, to promote social evolution along the natural lines of the race. We should not try to impress our ideas in upon them in a flood, but help them to advance in their own way. In other words, our object must be to make them not Americans but civilized Malays.

The two problems are quite distinct, and each presents its peculiar difficulties. One is that of a subtropical island whose inhabitants, although foreigners, are largely of European blood. The other is that of a tropical country, peopled almost entirely by Asiatics. The English have shown in India, and in the still closer parallel of the Malay Peninsula, that the Philippine problem can be solved. They have shown that peoples not unlike the Tagals, the Visayans and the Moros can be ruled successfully; and our difficulty lies in the fact that we have yet to learn the art, and must display the self-restraint required to practice it. The difficulty here is not so much to find out how the thing ought to be done, as to do it; while in Porto Rico the opposite is true.

There historical examples are of negative rather than of positive value. In the cases most nearly analogous there were conditions that simplified matters, and England adopted, as I shall try to show, a solution that is hardly open to us. The Philippinos are utterly incapable of ruling themselves in a civilized way, so that there need be no question about the need of obtaining the consent of the governed, to distract us in the pursuit of their welfare; but in Porto Rico the political aspirations of the people cannot be disregarded, and it will probably not be easy to reconcile these with our views of the best policy for the island. The difference is like that of managing a small child and a half-grown man. A wise parent does what is best for the child, and makes him obey; but the lad must be allowed a pass-key, and yet is not given control of his property.

If we are constrained to undertake the management of Cuba, the problem will be like that of Porto Rico and will present similar difficulties.

THE PHILIPPINES.

The task here is that of ruling a tropical colony, where the proportion of white men must always remain insignificant, and where the natives, except in the case of selected individuals, will be incapable of taking part in the government for an indefinite period. The most important requisites for the administration of such a colony are justice, a consistent policy, and a thorough knowledge of the native character. The first of these will probably be best attained by the methods pursued in all English-speaking countries, the methods which the English have generally adopted in ruling Asiatics, that of placing alongside the higher administrative officials independent judicial tribunals. It must inevitably happen that local officials are sometimes given judicial powers, but in such cases there ought to be an appeal to the supreme court of the colony, so composed that one or more of the members shall be versed in the common law and others thoroughly familiar with the native customs. Such a court cannot be created in a day, but with care it could be brought to perfection before long.

Not less indispensable are a consistent policy, and knowledge of native character. The need of the last of these is self-evident, and in regard to the former it is clear that nothing will destroy the confidence and respect of the native more quickly than any appearance of vacillation. Now England, the greatest of all colonizing powers, and Holland, the next most successful, have both sought to attain these objects by treating their colonial officials as a distinct permanent service, and offering an assured career to every man who entered it, and it is hard to see how the result can be reached in any other way. A knowledge of the native character and conditions is not one of those things that comes from Yankee shrewdness, or skill in operating the political machine. It requires long residence on the spot. France has made the mistake of selecting her colonial officials from the home administrative service, and sending them to the colonies as a step in the line of their promotion. Leroy-Beaulieu, the first of French authorities on colonies, laments this practice of his countrymen, and it has certainly been one of the causes of their lack of success. We must remember, also, that service in the tropics is far from healthy, and if the proper kind of man is to be secured the pay must be liberal, and the incumbent must be able to look forward to a pension that will enable him to spend the rest of his life comfortably at home after devoting his best years to the work of the colony. Entrance into the service ought, of course, to be conditioned upon proof of qualification. The English make their examinations for the Indian civil service of such a nature as to admit only men of liberal education, and encourage the successful candidates to spend their two years of probation at one of the universities. They have felt the great importance of bringing to bear upon colonial administration the highest and broadest culture that the mother country can produce —certainly an excellent method of making European civilization a potent influence in the East. Probably the best way of recruiting our colonial service would be to establish an academy like West Point or Annapolis. The system has proved most admirable for the army and navy, and ought to be equally good for another technical occupation. It has shown itself in harmony with our institutions. It gives sufficient play to the American love of patronage, by the mode of selecting the candidates for admission, while it produces a service strongly imbued with the best professional traditions. West Point and Annapolis have been both popular and efficient, and good sense would suggest an extension of the principle.

That the colonial administration ought to be independent of party politics in America, that the governor-general of the Philippines ought not to be a party hack who is not big enough for a position in the Cabinet, needs no demonstration. In fact the success of England as a colonial power dates from the time when the administration of her colonies was divorced from party struggles in Parliament. It is no less evident that the governor-general ought to be advised by a council drawn from the wisest officials in his colony. There is, however, another principle which is less obvious. It is that of avoiding excessive interference from home. Lord Durham in his famous report on the government of Canada in 1839 commented severely upon this evil from which the colonies had suffered long. It is a danger that is much increased by the telegraph, and one to which the United States is peculiarly exposed. Any one familiar with the national administration must be aware how highly centralized, or as the French say concentrated, it is. The postmaster of one of our large cities can hardly get a radiator shifted or a wall painted, until permission has been obtained from Washington. Now such a state of things is utterly inconsistent with good colonial administration, for the home authorities are only dimly informed of colonial conditions, and cannot by means of any amount of dispatches, reports and cable messages be made thoroughly familiar with them. The governor on the spot must be allowed a large measure of discretion in all matters that do not involve things outside the colony. But it takes a great deal of experience to learn to leave the local officials a free hand, for the home government is easily affected by the representations of interested parties, who are able to display an amount of local knowledge that is quite overwhelming. In England, where the whole system of parliamentary government depends upon the observance of conventions and upon mutual forbearance, the difficulty is less than in America, where we are more accustomed in politics to exert our legal rights. It would seem wise, therefore, to define the authority of the governor by law, so that only matters of grave concern should be reserved for decision at home.

The employment of capable, influential natives by the government is a matter of no little consequence. It secures their loyalty, and bridges over the gap between the rulers and the ruled. No doubt the mainstay of the administration in the Philippines must be found in the American officials, but many of the minor posts and magistracies can, as in India, be filled with natives, and a few of the most capable could probably be given seats on the governor's council. Native troops under American officers could also be employed—a proceeding that tends to make good subjects of restless spirits, and lessens the number of American soldiers that have to be kept in a tropical climate. Our negro troops will save us from maintaining the proportion of white men in the tropics that England is obliged to keep there, but still they might well be supplemented by Philippinos.

This leads naturally to the suggestion, often made of late, of governing through the native chiefs, as Great Britain has done in India and the Malay Peninsula. That such a system is advantageous wherever practicable, English experience amply proves; and indeed, it is now a maxim in India that every native state ought to be preserved with scrupulous care. To what extent the system can be applied in the Archipelago, what islands and districts bear such an allegiance to a native chief that he can maintain authority over them, is a question on which only men with a rare familiarity with the different tribes can venture an opinion. The most promising subject for experiment would seem to be the Sultan of Sulu. In the general form which the system has now reached in India the native princes can hold communication with each other, and with foreign powers, only through the Indian government. Their military forces are limited. They cannot take white men into their service without permission. They must allow the British to move troops, place garrisons and camps, and build railways and post roads in their territories. Successions to the throne are not valid until recognized by the viceroy, who can intervene in case of rebellion or gross misrule, and in extreme cases can depose the prince and appoint another. More important than all the rest the British resident accredited to the prince, watches his administration, gives him advice, and exerts a constant if unobtrusive pressure in favor of good government. The system has been especially successful where a long minority has given the resident an opportunity to educate the young prince, and administer his estates in his name until he has come of age.

The tendency on the whole has been, while exalting the dignity of the princes, to bring them more and more into harmony with the policy of the empire. The system relieves England of a load of responsibility, and at the same time removes discontent, by giving to a large part of India the satisfaction of native rule, and enabling the Hindoos under direct British government to realize how well they are treated. With the federated Malay states the connection is much closer, for although these states are spoken of as "protected" by England, they are now virtually governed directly by her agents. In the treaty of 1895 the rulers of the Malay states agreed to follow the advice of the British resident-general in all matters of administration, other than those touching the Mohammedan religion, and by this fiction he is enabled to carry on the government in their name.

It is, perhaps, needless to emphasize the importance of absolute religious toleration. We believe in it, and practice it, so fully at home that we are not likely to violate it in our dependencies. But there is another question that demands immediate and far-seeing consideration. I refer to the immigration of Chinese. As soon as order has been restored, and a measure of prosperity created, they are likely to come in great numbers; and they will be heartily welcomed by the foreign capitalists, because they supply an abundance of industrious and cheap laborers. But their presence will undoubtedly have the same results as in the Straits Settlements and Sarawak, where their superior thrift, industry and commercial aptitude has placed all the smaller trade in their hands, and thus they have prospered at the expense of the Malays, who would, it is said, massacre them all with the greatest satisfaction if the Pax Britannica were removed. The Chinese are utterly impervious to European civilization, regarding it simply as a protection under which they can thrive, and whether it is wise, or right toward the natives, to suffer such an element to increase in the Archipelago for the sake of their labor is at least extremely doubtful. · Moreover, it will be invidious to forbid the people of our own dependency to come to our shores. The Philippinos are not fond enough of hard work to make their immigration to the United States in considerable numbers anything but a nightmare of the labor unions, but the Chinese will miss no channel for getting here that is left unstopped. We have already prohibited Chinese immigration to Hawaii, and we must consider at once the question whether we will permit it to the Philippines.

PORTO RICO.

Porto Rico presents, as I have said, peculiar difficulties of its own. At first sight the problem appears simple enough. The obvious solution is to establish there a government like that of one of our territories, with a government appointed by the President, and a legislature elected by the people. This system has worked very well here; but we have tried it only as a temporary expedient, a stepping-stone to statehood. It has lasted only while the population was thinly scattered. When a territory has become settled densely enough to be a real community, with a political life of its own, it has been admitted as a state. Now Porto Rico is almost as densely peopled to-day as any part of the United States, and yet it must be clear that it cannot be admitted as a state until it has been trained in self-government, and has acquired the political, social and industrial habits that prevail in the United States. That this will take a very great length of time every observer of political history will recognize. In short, the period is so long that statehood is too remote to be taken into consideration in determining the immediate administration of the island.

As a permanent method of colonial government, or one that is intended to last for any great length of time, the system of a governor appointed by the mother country and a legislature elected by the colony is open to grave objections. Continual struggles between these two authorities are almost inevitable, for the legislature naturally wants to have its way, and where it is thwarted by the governor it learns to look upon him as the representative of an alien if not a hostile power; and yet the governor must sometimes check the legislature unless the colony is to be given virtual independence. The system tends, therefore, to promote friction instead of the mutual sympathy that ought to exist between the parent state and the colony. England tried it, and after many bitter experiences, was forced to discard it. She tried it with her North American colonies, and the consequences were constant bickerings, until the Revolution cut the connection altogether. She tried it in Canada with similar results, which culminated in the rebellion of 1837. The remedy in this case was found in the granting of responsible government, that is, in placing the governor-general in a position like that of the Queen, and transferring the real exercise of his powers to ministers responsible to the popular chamber of the colony. Except for foreign relations Canada thus became independent in almost everything but name. Finally England tried it in the case of Jamaica, and the contests with the legislature that ensued were not terminated until the people of the island, terrified by the insurrection of the negroes in 1865, voluntarily gave up their constitution, and the elected legislature was replaced by one appointed by the Crown. Warned by these experiences, England changed her policy, and granted responsible government as fast as possible to all her colonies where men of English race were numerous. She even pressed it upon Australia and the Cape before they were anxious to receive it. All the North American and Australian colonies and Cape Colony and Natal have now full responsible government; while of the other dependencies that have any representative element in their constitution, only three, Bermuda, the Bahamas and Barbados, have a purely elective legislative chamber, and these three are small and peculiarly situated. In all the rest (Jamaica, Guiana, the Leeward Islands, Mauritius, Cyprus and Malta) the legislative council is partly elected and partly appointed, usually in such proportions that the appointed members form at least one-half of the body. England has learned not to create an elective legislature unless she is prepared to go farther in a short time and grant to the colony complete control of its affairs, and thus a distinction has arisen, which tends to become sharper and sharper, between Crown colonies and self-governing colonies.

If this is true of colonies whose people are of English race, emigrants from the United Kingdom, it must be manifestly far more true where the population of the colony differs from the bulk of that of the parent, or rather adopting, state by race, by religion, and by political traditions. Yet that is the case in Porto Rico. The nearest parallel to the condition that confronts us there is to be found in the history of French Canada, and the most valuable study of the problems it presents is the report of Lord Durham, made after the rebellion of 1837. This document, to which I have already referred, pointed out forcibly the evils that had flowed from placing side by side an elected legislature and a governor with real authority, and it urged the necessity of establishing responsible government in the colony. Although Canada had then been under English rule for about eighty years, and had had an elective assembly for nearly half a century, the training of the French Canadians in self-government would hardly have been enough to make the remedy suggested practicable had it not been for the vast tracts of waste land which brought a great influx of English settlers. In fact the province of Upper Canada, which was united with the French province by the act of 1840, was entirely English. Now the people of Porto Rico are not very much less lacking in political experience than the French Canadians were at the capture of Quebec, and there is no vacant territory into which Americans can move in great numbers. Hence responsible government in the English sense cannot safely be set up for a long time to come, and the island must first undergo a period of apprenticeship. Moreover, our own people are quite unfamiliar with the conceptions that underlie the principles of responsible government, and they would fail to understand the position of a governor who, on the ground that his legal powers were in the safe keeping of a colonial cabinet, sanctioned unwise and unjust laws, or a hostile tariff, enacted by the colonial legislature. If the governor is to exert no real authority it would probably be wiser to cast the island adrift, providing only that it should hold no communication with the outside world save through the President of the United States. This would, no doubt, involve complications with foreign powers, but at least it would be a system that our people could comprehend. The island would then be a protected state and not a dependency. It would be a Spanish-American republic whose foreign relations alone would be under the guardianship of the United States. Perhaps this would be the most prudent relation for us to hold with the island, and a great deal could be said on both sides of that question.

Assuming, however, as the title of this discussion indicates, that Porto Rico is to remain a dependency of this country, it would seem that an elected assembly with general legislative powers cannot wisely be established. If that is true, two courses are open to us. An elected assembly with strictly limited powers may be created, other matters being reserved for the governor and an appointed council; or the English example may be followed of vesting general legislative powers in a body composed partly of appointed and partly of elected members, the latter, say a dozen in number, being perhaps chosen by the seven provinces. The second plan, at least at the outset, would probably be the safer with a people unused to constitutional limitations. But in any event the appointed members of the governor's council ought to be selected from residents, and as far as possible, from natives of the island. By this process, jealousy of foreign rule could be minimized, for the mere fact that the chief officials were appointed ought not to be seriously obnoxious to the inhabitants, who are not accustomed to any other method of selection.

I am aware that the powers entrusted to the governor and council may be abused, although the danger is surely no greater than in the case of a popular assembly elected by a people unused to self-government. But I do not think we need to fear a repetition of the carpet-bag rule. That was made possible only by the disorganized and distracted state of the south; and by the sudden enfranchisement of an enormous mass of untrained voters, at a time when the North distrusted every Southerner who had the slightest experience of public affairs. It may be observed, also, that where the political conditions are such as to permit the existence of carpet-bag rule, the presence of an elected assembly tends rather to aggravate than to remove the evil; and further, that if we appoint governors of the carpet-bag type, they will wreck any system of government that can be devised.

The development of local self-government is a matter of the highest importance, for it is the foundation of true political liberty. Capacity for popular government cannot be created by edict. It must be acquired by slow experience, and efforts to produce it suddenly have usually been disastrous. It requires the gradual training of large numbers of men to the conduct of public affairs on a small scale; and not less a strong reverence for the authority of law, as distinguished from the commands of men. Hence it must begin with local government administered under strict rules of law. Lord Durham remarked the defective municipal organization of Canada, and laid stress in his report upon the necessity of improving it. We ought to foster by every means in our power the management of local affairs in Porto Rico by the people themselves, and in doing so it would be well to follow as nearly as possible the existing forms and institutions, filling them with a more vigorous spirit. It may be necessary at first to appoint the alcalde, or mayor, but he should be selected from among the leading citizens of the commune, and should be assisted by a council elected on some qualification based on property or education, which will insure that the electorate shall not be an ignorant and credulous mass of voters. The franchise could easily be so arranged that it should gradually expand automatically as prosperity and education increased. The general principles of local self-government once fixed, their application will no doubt be tentative for some time to come, and it is certainly presumptuous for anyone unfamiliar with life on the island to attempt to talk about details.

A permanent civil service is essential in Porto Rico as well as in the Philippines, although it would have a somewhat different character. In the Philippines we must depend in the main on American officials, while in Porto Rico the service ought, after the first few years, to be recruited almost exclusively from the natives. The reason why the spoils system has not proved even more intolerable in the United States must be sought in the extraordinary versatility of the American, and in the general diffusion of education. But these qualities are wanting in the inhabitants of Porto Rico, and therefore if we are to have the support of an efficient administrative force, we must have a permanent and well-trained civil service. The United States cannot afford to throw away any chances in the difficult and untried task before it.

The judicial system is perhaps the most important point of all. If the people of Porto Rico are to acquire our political ideas and traditions it must be chiefly by means of the courts of law, for the relation of the courts to the administrative officials and to the citizens is the fundamental point of difference between the Anglo-Saxon system of government and that of the Latin races. It is the force that prevents the government from being autocratic, that makes it a government of laws and not of men. Porto Rico can never obtain our political system unless she first becomes thoroughly familiar with our judicial conceptions. I do not mean that the substantive law needs to be changed. On the contrary, some branches of the law must obviously be retained, and nothing would be gained by changing most of the others. To change the law of land is oppressive, while commercial law, the law of contracts and so forth, are very much alike over the whole civilized world. England had to decide the same question when she conquered Canada, and after an unfortunate effort to introduce the common law, she determined, in the Quebec Act of 1774, to substitute the English criminal law as being milder than the French at that time, but to leave the Canadian law in other respects untouched. Porto Rico has now the civil law, and it had better not be disturbed except so far as it may be amended in detail from time to time by legislation. There is no difficulty in administering the civil law by means of the American judicial system. The common law has always recognized the binding force of local customs, and there has never been any trouble in the case of Louisiana, which still retains the civil law as the basis of her jurisprudence. Incidentally the maintenance of the existing law would avoid any question about juries in civil suits,—if the provision about jury trial in the Constitution applies to Porto Rico at all,—because in civil cases the provision extends only to suits at common law. It does not apply to equity causes or to litigation under the civil law.

The important thing is that the organization and authority of the American courts should be planted in Porto Rico, together with the method of procedure and the rules of evidence. The best judicial organization would probably be that under which the common law was successfully built up; local courts with a limited jurisdiction, and a central court for the whole island, which should hear appeals in bank, and whose members should go on circuit through the several provinces. They could be assisted in ascertaining the facts in any case by local assessors or the local magistrates. No system better adapted for maintaining the dignity of the courts and the authority of the law has ever been devised. It would appear wise also to allow appeals in certain cases to the Supreme Court at Washington, although such appeals would not be numerous. England has always permitted an appeal from her colonial courts to the Judicial

Committee of the Privy Council, which is to-day virtually the same court as the House of Lords, the highest tribunal of the United Kingdom. Such an appeal is useful in many ways. It tends to unify the law, and to preserve the authority of the parent state without the irritation that might be provoked by action of the executive department. Moreover, it acts as a restraint on all public bodies and functionaries in the colony to know that the legality of their acts is liable to be called in question before a paramount power, the greatest tribunal of the parent state.

A potent force in fostering the affection of the people of Porto Rico for the United States might be found in the army and the navy. Not only might the natives of the island be recruited into the ranks, but a certain number of promising young men might receive Presidential appointments year by year to West Point and Annapolis, just as commissions in the British army are now reserved for young colonials. There is certainly nothing that stimulates loyalty to a flag so much as serving under it.

The regulation of the grant of concessions or franchises will be a thorny problem in both our dependencies, for the danger of abuse is exceeding great. England encountered the same question in the form of the disposition of crown lands in the colonies; and we know a little about it ourselves from some trifling experiences at home. The only safeguard we have yet discovered is to provide that such grants shall not be made by special acts, but by general law alone; and although that principle cannot be strictly applied to the gigantic corporations bred by economy of operation in a huge country, it can probably be applied in our new possessions for many years to come.

One more suggestion before closing, for suggestions are singularly easy to make when one has no responsibility for carrying them out. There would seem to be no motive for haste in creating civil governments either for Porto Rico or the Philippines. The military rule in Porto Rico appears to be proceeding smoothly, and in the Archipelago civil government cannot be established until order is restored. There are certainly cases where it is more important to act right than to act quickly.

THE GOVERNMENT OF TROPICAL COLONIES.

W. ALLEYNE IRELAND, ESQ., *London, England.*

It is a curious instance of the mutability of human affairs that three years ago the United States should have practically threatened war against England on account of an alleged attempt on the part of the latter to extend the boundaries of one of her colonies and that to-day the United States should be taking heart of grace in her colonial ventures from England's colonial successes. I mention this merely to show how entirely foreign to the American mind was any idea of territorial expansion a couple of years ago. Perhaps there could be named no subject on which the people at large in this country possess so little information as the government of dependencies; nothing could be more natural. It could never have been contemplated that the government of dependencies would ever be a problem which the people of the United States would be called on to face. Since it became evident that the Philippine Islands and Porto Rico would have to be governed by American administration a vast amount of rubbish has appeared in the newspapers of the country in reference to the nature of the problem thus suddenly arising out of the success of American arms. Articles have appeared in even the more respectable journals in reference to the colonial system of England which contained inaccuracies which would be severely punished in an English schoolboy of fourteen years of age. It has become common to refer to England's colonial empire as though it consisted of a number of homogeneous parts which in the main present to the sovereign state problems of a similar nature. Nothing could be farther from the facts, and I am inclined to think that before any good work can be done in the direction of educating public sentiment in regard to the government of Porto Rico and the Philippines the fact must be clearly established that the government of tropical dependencies is a very different question from the government of states or dependencies outside the tropics. In a tropical climate the conditions of life are so different from any that can be found in northern countries that the experience of home government forms a poor guide for colonial administration. In Europe and in North America the task of government is made comparatively easy from the fact that the general tendency of the majority of the people is in the direction of progress, industry, social improvement, morality and good order; and every act of the government which does not injuriously affect any of these factors meets with the approval and active support of the masses. In tropical climates, on the other hand, the aims of the government find but little encouragement amongst the masses. The population contains but a small element of that material which is necessary for progressive development, and color prejudice forms an insuperable barrier to the social advancement of that small minority of the colored race which succeeds in attaining positions of honorable independence. By far the greater number of individuals in tropical countries are without any ambition to do more than secure the necessities of life, and the ease with which this ambition is satisfied contributes in no small degree to the idleness and indifference which is the marked characteristic of the population. A short residence in a tropical colony serves to convince most persons of the governing class of the utter hopelessness of effecting any material change in the natural disposition of the natives, and whether such conviction is based on insufficient grounds or not, the result is the same, and each successive generation of reformers faces the situation with an amazing confidence for a while and then wraps itself up in a garment of indifference, stifling any inconvenient pricks of conscience with the assurance that the time is not yet ripe for the wholesale regeneration of humanity. Thus it happens that the new governor, the new colonial secretary, the new administrator, be he never so bemedaled for worthiness in past service at home, sends to his government the same discouraging tale of a people possessing indeed some virtues of the lesser kind, but lost to all desire for progress and content to live a life in which no disturbing thought of rising above the common level intrudes on the soothing monotony of existence. No one who has spent any considerable time in the tropics can have failed to observe that where any degree of prosperity has been reached, where any approach to sanitary conditions exists, where, in fact, any indication of progress is in evidence, these things have been achieved not by means of but in spite of the mass of the people. That in some parts of the tropics this may be due in some degree to the evil effects of slavery constitutes a satisfactory excuse for those conditions, the existence of which is not in any way affected by a consideration of their origin. When measured by the commercial standard the difference between tropical and non-tropical colonies becomes most strikingly apparent. Thus taking England's tropical and non-tropical colonies I find that during the past five years the non-tropical colonies, Australia, Canada and Newfoundland, imported British produce to the value of $15.34 per head of their population, whilst the tropical colonies imported British goods to the value of only fifty-six cents per head. Again, the non-tropical colonies exported to England produce to the value of $22.88 per head and the tropical colonies produce to the value of sixty cents a head. During the past twelve years I have spent most of my time in the British colonies. I was for seven years in the West Indies and visited India and several of the French and Dutch tropical colonies. My observations during the past twelve years have led me to form opinions in regard to the tropics which are likely to be very unpopular in this country. I claim no authority for my opinions. If the conclusions at which I have arrived are wrong I can only say that they are the outcome of careful and unprejudiced investigation. I may say then that I do not believe that the inhabitants of the tropics will ever be capable of self-government in the sense which is usually attached to that expression. Is there at the present day to be found anywhere in the tropics a country which is showing itself capable of self-government? I might go farther and ask has there ever been any country in the tropics which has shown itself capable of self-government? It is true that in Peru at the time of the Incas there was a government which maintained discipline and order amongst the people of that country, but the government was autocratic and did not lay with the people, and excellent as the results of the system were in many respects, they have been very generally condemned by writers because they did not proceed from self-government, but from a perfect form of despotism. Now if we glance at India as it is to-day we see a spectacle of three hundred million people governed by thirty thousand British officials. There has been a great clamor in favor of India for the Indians. It is claimed and with great justice that the Hindoos, who have been educated according

THE GOVERNMENT OF DEPENDENCIES. 63

to western notions, have shown themselves capable of entering all the professions with the greatest credit to themselves in their examinations. I am free to admit that I have never met amongst other races men who have shown such an exquisite subtlety of intellect, such an extraordinary aptitude for learning, as some Hindoos whom I have known, but unfortunately subtlety of intellect does not help people toward self-government. It is a very common error to suppose that administrative capacity goes hand in hand with intellectual attainment. You may take a native official in India and as long as things run smoothly he will amaze you by the cleverness and ingenuity of his annual report; compared with it the unvarnished statements of his English brother official will appear as the crude production of a schoolboy. But send a flood, send a famine, devastate his territory with disease and what do you find, an absolute incapacity for action. Then it is that the administrative ability of the Englishman steps in and saves the country from disaster. What is wanted in the government of colonies is extreme energy and determination and these qualities are not found in the make-up of the oriental races. If we turn now to the negro in the tropics we find a still worse condition of affairs. In the British West Indies, where the negro is treated better than in any other part of the world, we find the negro voters sending negroes into the legislative assemblies—in some of these colonies the negro or colored men outnumber the white persons. For more than a year I attended all the meetings of the legislative assembly in such a colony. I listened hour upon hour to the speeches of these negro legislators. I found many of them excellent speakers and keen debaters, but I found also that they were entirely unfit for legislative duties. They seemed to be possessed of no sense of proportion, no sense of responsibility; they were apparently governed almost entirely by their emotions. It would appear as though the British colonial office held similar views to those which I have expressed, for within the past year two islands, Dominica and Tobago, have been deprived of their representative institutions; the former has been converted into a crown colony and the latter has been made a ward of Trinidad. Those who are best informed in the West Indies tell me that it is contemplated to make considerable changes in the near future in the government of the British West Indian colonies. Now it is often urged that the reason why the negro in the tropics has not shown himself capable of self-government is because he has not had time. If we take the case of the chief negro republic, Hayti, it would certainly appear that they have not had time, for it is beyond doubt a fact that cannibalism prevails to a considerable extent in the republic. Sir Spencer St. John in his book on Hayti, published in 1884, places the matter altogether beyond question and during a visit I paid to the island in 1893 I saw sufficient to convince me that the abominable practice still existed, but, as a matter of fact, the negroes have had just as much time to develop a civilization and to evolve a satisfactory form of government as the white man. There were negroes in Africa when Cæsar landed on British soil and since that time the people of Britain have made themselves what they are to-day whilst the negro in Africa remains substantially what he was. The reason why the negro has made no progress is that a tropical climate does not place a man under any necessity to exert himself, and there is no reason to suppose that the climatic influence of the tropics will be less powerful in the next thousand years than it has been in the past thousand years. I am inclined to think that so long as theorists will maintain that political and ethical principles have an universal applicability, so long will all attempts at civilizing the tropics end in grievous disappointment. I will not go so far as to say that the faculty of governing the tropics lies wholly with the Anglo-Saxon race but I am firmly of the opinion that without the strong hand of the man of the north to hold things together the tropics will never advance beyond the point which has been reached by the central American republics. James Anthony Froude has, to my mind, expressed the whole question of the government of tropical dependencies in the following lines, taken from his "English in the West Indies": "The leading of the wise few, the willing obedience of the many, is the beginning and end of all right action. Secure this, and you secure everything. Fail to secure it, and, be your liberties as wide as you can make them, no success is possible.

DISCUSSION.

DR. TALCOTT WILLIAMS, *Philadelphia*.

The discussion to which we have listened for three hours, has covered all three phases of this subject, constitutional, administrative and industrial, with a complete ability. We may fitly congratulate the Academy upon its series of papers, which face this national issue with confidence, accept its responsibilities without hesitation and see in our laws, our government and our citizenship the material for its successful solution.

The burden of utterance has been in favor of the constitutional power of the government to discharge all the duties before it in the administration of dependencies. This was also the case in the debate in Congress. While Professor Woolsey and Professor Huffcut confine themselves to this aspect, Professor Lowell has dealt in a strain as encouraging with the administrative necessities of the case, and the solitary doubt as to the future is raised by Mr. Ireland in his assertion, which I will take up later, that contract laws are indispensable in dealing with labor in the tropics.

The constitutional argument advanced by both Professor Woolsey and Professor Huffcut has become familiar during the last six months. They differ, one in believing that it will be necessary to adjust constitutional guarantees in some shape, and the other in asserting that they do not extend over territory newly acquired. I do not propose here and now to review this constitutional discussion, but I desire to draw attention to a phase of this branch of our subject, to which neither has alluded. In guessing on the future decisions of the Supreme Court, it has generally proved wiser to trust to the trend of its past history than to our analysis of its probable reasons for a future decision. For a century, since its early decisions first struck out the path, the Supreme Court, with the exception of the solitary decision in the Dred Scott case has never found a national need without discovering a national power. This has been the basis of its steady extension of the powers of the "federal agency" into the prerogatives of a nation possessing all the powers required in the external discharge of its duties in the field of international law. In deciding internal questions the pendulum of the Supreme Court has swung from one extreme to the other, but in deciding those questions created by the external relations of the United States, ending in the luminous decisions in Ross' case, quoted by Professor Huffcut (140 U. S.

453), the Supreme Court has always found whatever power it was necessary for the United States to have to act in its sovereign capacity. I need not review these cases. They have decided the right to acquire territory, to determine its government, to govern territory conquered, but not annexed, to enforce treaties, to exclude aliens in time of peace and to discharge, even to the execution and imprisonment of American citizens, the civil and criminal jurisdictions of ex-territorial law in Oriental countries. With this clear ascending curve running through a century, it is no great stretch of either imagination or calculation to assume that the Supreme Court will reach a precisely similiar conclusion when it is called upon to decide whether the nation organized by the constitution can exercise the ordinary national powers of other nations in dealing with annexed territory.

The precise letter of the constitution of course, blocks the way, as Professor Woolsey has pointed out. Through it, Professor Huffcut has driven his ingenious tunnel, but the provision in regard to jury duty is in the same article with the provision in regard to judges holding for good behavior, and if Congress can establish courts which can legally condemn a man when the judge only holds for a term of years in our territories, it could by parity of reasoning eliminate the jury. Nor is this all. The United States has had three successive classes of territory acquired, first from cession by states to the United States, under conditions which the Supreme Court has recognized as limiting congressional action, second by the cession of foreign countries under treaties which stipulated that in the new acquisitions, the citizens of the ceding nation should enjoy the privileges of the citizens of the nation accepting the cession, which Justice Marshall held the sole basis of civil rights. Third, our present acquisitions which are ceded without this provision and in which by implication these rights are not conferred by annexation. There is here a steady sequence whose march and progress the Supreme Court sought to interrupt in the Dred Scott decision, but in which the arbitrament of events proved more powerful than the logic of Taney. The absence of this treaty clause in our last acquisitions under the reasoning of Marshall vitally changes the situation, and while it does not alter the power of Congress to legislate, it changes the environment under which it acts.

Any confusion on this subject arises from failing to discriminate between the limits of sovereignty and constitutional jurisdiction. The decisions in the California cases to which Professor Huffcut alluded (Cross *v.* Harrison, 16 Howard, 164) do not base the right to levy taxes on the war power, but the absence of constitutional reason for interference with these taxes on the fact that Congress had not yet legislated so as to extend the jurisdiction of the laws of the United States, its treaties and its constitution. Sovereignty and jurisdiction may be coterminous. Either may exist where the other is absent. The sovereignty of the United States sentenced in Japan to death and provided for the imprisonment of Ross for life in Albany, a stronger case than the finding in Japan because the sentence had to be executed within our constitutional limits, but no one will pretend that the constitutional jurisdiction of the United States applied in either case because if it had a jury would have been necessary, and the Supreme Court wisely found the authority for dealing with the life and liberty of an American citizen, not in any special grant of power to Congress, but in the necessity for the exercise of the international powers of an independent sovereignty. A long series of decisions show that the executive sovereignty of the English crown attaches at the instant of conquest, but the judicial jurisdiction of the English crown only begins after an order in council has extended it. The sovereignty of the United States extends over an Indian tribe ; but its members are not within the constitutional jurisdiction of the United States and the right of Congress to regulate the manner in which the local powers of such a tribe shall be exercised does not render such local powers Federal powers, arising from and created by the Constitution of the United States. (Tatton *v.* Mayer, 163 U. S. 376.) By discovery the sovereignty of the United States extended over the Guano Islands which our citizens occupy, but the jurisdiction of the United States is only established there by act, and if Congress instead of making Navassa a ship as it did by section 5516 R. S. had given its governor power of life and death the grant would have rested on as complete constitutional power in one case as in the other. National sovereignty exists complete, unchallenged and unquestioned over the Philippine Islands and Porto Rico. The authority now exercised there is ordinarily spoken of as the war power of the President, but it is also the necessary exercise, as the Supreme Court pointed out in the case already cited, of that authority which attaches to a sovereignty that acquires territory, an authority which is not provided for in the constitution, but which exists as a logical deduction from the fact that the constitution created a sovereignty with complete national powers for international purposes.

The constitution created a constitutional jurisdiction within certain definite limits, to wit, the states which formed the union. It also created a nation with the usual international powers needed and demanded by an independent nation, recognized and acting as such under the law of nations. To both of these propositions all agree.

When this national sovereignty acts within the sphere of constitutional jurdisdiction, it is limited by constitutional provisions. When as a national sovereignty, it acts within the international field, it has whatever powers are needed for its work as such, a principle established by a long series of decisions. (Fong Yue Ting *v.* U. S. 149, U. S. 712). Sovereignty is exercised over conquered territory under no specific constitutional power, but as part of the rights inherent in the international nation created by the constitution. Legislation, by treaty or statute (American Insurance Co. *v.* Canter, 1 Peters, 511), decides when the constitutional jurisdiction shall be coterminous with this national sovereignty, and until some legislation, treaty or statute decides this political question, the judicial power of the United States does not attach (Jecker *v.* Montgomery, 13 Howard, 498); unless Congress legislates otherwise, the "belligerent rights of a conqueror" remaining complete until this time (16 Howard, 164). Sovereignty, in short, moves with the international acts of the nation. Constitutional jurisdiction travels with the municipal law of the United States, and is created by a treaty because it is part of that law. Nor does any decision, not even that cited referring to the District of Columbia, traverse this distinction, for the simple reason, if no other, that a treaty annexing territory without conferring civil rights—that is, extending constitutional jurisdiction in greater or less degree—has never yet been before our courts. I submit, therefore, that in dealing with territory thus annexed, there may be found a power wider than that simply "to make all needful rules and regulations respecting territory, and other property," to wit, that broader national power which permits annexation itself, though the constitution makes no provision for the act and under which power a long series of statutes have been passed and even juryless courts created as part of national sovereignty, and not part of our municipal constitutional jurisdiction.

In dealing with the administration of dependencies, Professor Lowell has laid stress, as is indeed fit, on the trained and organized character of the English colonial service. But the precise force and efficacy of the English colonial administration is and always has attached to the absence of this requirement in its higher parts. It is the combination of a trained force headed and controlled by men chosen from the general political life of the realm and for political service which gives the English colonial service practical efficiency. A pure bureaucracy, a trained and examined colonial service, exclusively applied to colonial administration ends where the German colonial service, which is of this character, has always ended, in the perpetual broils and the perpetual blunders of the "competition wallah," if he has not some one over him selected by the competition of life and not of examination. Ultimate power in India rests with the governor-general and governors of the presidencies, men selected from active English political life, and for these posts a Conservative government, selects Conservatives and a Liberal administration, Liberals. Sir Alfred Milner, the ablest figure to-day in English colonial administration, was a dozen years ago a mere journalist and has never gone through the competition mill. Of the seven Australian governors last year only two had ever had political training. The rest had been, one a gentleman in waiting, another groom of the chambers, another "Verderer of Epping Forest"—an ancient office doubtless, but whose direct training for colonial administration must be admitted to be slender by the few, even in this audience, who can define its duties. A successful explorer, like Thomson, a good regimental officer, some journalist or barrister with a genius for management, a man successful in English politics—these have made half the good colonial governors, aided and supported by a trained force selected by competition as their administrative tools.

Nor are Anglo-Indian salaries what they were. The very place Macaulay took to accumulate a competence, can to-day be held only by a man with a private fortune to bridge the gap between the salary paid and the level of expenditure demanded by the post.

Mr. Alleyne Ireland speaks the undoubted conviction of all Englishmen in deeming contract labor laws necessary in the tropics. I may be pardoned if I remember that every English paper teemed with this advice thirty-three years ago, in behalf of the cotton crop. We were assured—Who does not remember it?—that without contract laws the negro would not work and the cotton crop cease. Our largest crop then had been 3,000,000 bales. Free labor has quadrupled the yield. There are two ways of making a man work—by pressure from above, disguised slavery—or by stimulus from within, the higher wages of a highly organized, free, industrial system. The last, the tropics have never yet had. Jamaica and the other English tropical West Indian Islands are the dissevered fragments of a continent from whose industrial activity they have been separated. Give the stimulus of a market and of high wages and all men will work. Deprive them of either and contract labor laws are needed. The American may yet solve the tropical industrial problem as he has quadrupled the cotton crop in face of all the arguments marshaled by Mr. Ireland, all made thirty-three years ago, not by laws making it harder for a man to be idle but by an industrial system making it more profitable for a man to labor.

Professor L. S. ROWE, *University of Pennsylvania.*

It is no small task to add anything to the admirable addresses we have heard this afternoon. In them we find exhausted the possibilities of political organization in the management of dependencies, as well as the constitutional difficulties that we are likely to encounter. Upon these two questions—of political organization and constitutional interpretation—I wish to say a few words.

I have not the slightest doubt, that so far as the organization of government in our new dependencies is concerned, we shall be able —whether in Cuba, Porto Rico, or the Philippines—to adapt our standards to the needs and possibilities of the inhabitants of the islands. Arguing from precedent, there is reason to believe that our government will be too despotic rather than too free. It is a mistake to suppose that the extension of American rule means equality of political rights. Throughout our history the principle for which we have stood above all others is the maintenance of order and security. To this end we are prepared to subordinate all other political ideals and principles.

The real difficulties which we will encounter in the government of our new possessions, difficulties which are as yet new to us, lie in the field of the private rather than in that of the public law. In other words, while we shall in all likelihood be able to develop a governmental organization strong enough to meet any emergency, there is grave danger that by suddenly undermining customs, traditions and systems of law which do not conform to the principles of the common law, we shall destroy the fabric of social organization in the new territories. Incomplete and inadequate as such social organization may be, it is the first step in orderly, progressive development. To destroy it is to invite disintegration and decay. This danger is evidently very much greater in the Philippines than in either Cuba or Porto Rico. In the latter our first and most important mission is to reorganize the judicial system and the administration of law rather than its form. In certain departments of legal procedure— particularly that of land transfer—glaring abuses must be corrected. The only immediate change necessary in the substantive law however is to make it definite. We cannot afford to permit our Governor-General to indulge in the arbitrary interference with the form of law and administration of justice which characterized the rule of his Spanish predecessor. Under our rule, Cubans and Porto Ricans must be assured of equality before the law not only as between themselves, but also as against the public authorities. This does not mean that we must sweep away all local customary law and establish the code of the civil law throughout the islands, thus sacrificing efficiency to uniformity. If we will but keep in mind how easily the legal fibre of a people is undermined, how gradually permanent changes in legal standards are effected, we shall be spared many humiliating failures.

Our policy in Cuba and Porto Rico is comparatively simple when compared with the difficulties which we shall encounter in the Philippines. We shall there require a combination of firmness and forbearance which no nation has as yet shown in its dealings with inferior races. For it must be remembered that it was only after a series of bitter lessons that England acquired the first rudimentary notions as to the proper method of dealing with half-civilized peoples. In the Philippines we shall have to deal with almost every conceivable form of primitive institution, from the patriarchal family to the most pronounced theocracy. However their system may violate our legal standards, we must remember that it cannot be suddenly changed without setting the population adrift toward anarchy and rebellion. For a long time we may have to tolerate institutions that may seem undesirable, even unjust to our eyes, and yet which are absolutely necessary to maintain the cohesion of the present social system. Law of some kind is better than no law at all. If we endeavor suddenly to inject American ideas into Malay tribal relations, disintegration and disorder are certain to result. The most that we can hope to do at present is to prevent the more violent forms of tribal or individual aggression, to establish an equitable system of taxation and then allow the civilizing influence of industrial reorganization to pave the way for improvement in property and other legal relations. As Mr. Lowell has well said, we shall probably make many blunders, but it is asking too much to expect an easy solution to so complex and delicate a problem.

A word before closing, on the vexed question of constitutional interpretation. In this respect I am inclined to take quite a different view of the situation from that outlined by Professor Woolsey. If instead of analyzing the letter of constitutional interpretation, we stop to examine its spirit, we find one cardinal principle guiding the court, viz., to avoid as far as possible any interference with the political organs of the government on broad questions of public policy. In order to carry out this principle we find the court resorting to legal fictions, as for instance in Fleming v. Page, * and Hamilton v. Dillin.†

I am fully aware that this proposition in the general form may give rise to some misunderstanding. Is it not the function of the judiciary,

---

* 9 Howard, 603.
† 21 Wallace, 73.

ary, it will be asked, to safeguard the constitution and in so doing to check the action of the other organs of government? An analysis of the decisions of the Supreme Court will show that while this is true, it is subject to certain definite limitations. The court has consistently refused to interfere with what it calls "the political functions of the government."

While it has given no definite meaning to the term "political functions" the end which the court has kept in view seems quite clear, viz., to refrain from interfering with the political organs of the government whenever the peace, or safety of the country is endangered or the order and security of any district menaced. It would take us far beyond the limits of this discussion to examine the instances in which this principle has been carried out. The most striking cases have arisen in periods of conflict, such as the Civil and Mexican Wars. The Reconstruction Period was particularly fruitful in this respect.*

This desire to avoid conflict with the political organs of government has demanded a degree of self-restraint on the part of the judiciary which has aroused the admiration of every student of politics. This self-restraint has indirectly increased the authority of the courts, for it has assured to them the respect and support of the people in those cases in which the courts have seen fit to place checks upon executive action. Traditions such as these make it seem tolerably certain that the courts will not force upon the political organs of the government a construction of the constitution which would make good government in the Philippines impossible.

But what is the nature of this construction for which Professor Woolsey contends? Because, in Callan *v*. Wilson† the court held that the framers of the constitution were anxious to secure the benefits of the common law system to the whole people and, by implication, extended the right of trial by jury to the inhabitants of the District of Columbia, therefore, it is argued, this right must be extended to all the territory over which the United States may acquire dominion. This reasoning would apply to the amendments as well as to the body of the constitution. In order to avoid giving to the Filipinos the "right to keep and bear arms,"‡ and to guard against the dangers involved in guaranteeing to them the common law jury system, it is necessary to resort to a form of casuistry which can only be regarded as a subter-

---

* See Mississippi *v.* Johnson, 4 Wallace, 475; Georgia *v.* Stanton, 6 Wallace, 50; also Dunning "Essays on the Civil War and Reconstruction." Macmillan; 1898.
† 127 U. S. 540.
‡ Amendments, Article II.

fuge. In Cross *v.* Harrison* the court held that the President as commander-in-chief of the army might govern newly acquired territory and that such territory did not become domesticated until Congress had established a civil government. Arguing from the letter of this decision, it is held that so long as the President governs the Philippines under the provisional form of military administration, the constitutional guarantees will not attach. In other words, if this mode of interpretation be correct we are driven to the conclusion that in order to govern the Philippines efficiently we must establish irresponsible government with its attendant evil—civil government by the military arm. To preserve order and maintain liberty we must create one of the worst forms of despotism.

I dwell upon this point, for it seems to me to involve a serious menace to the orderly development of our institutions. If we must resort to such devices to "beat" the constitution, it will not be long before its authority will be seriously undermined. Many of those who believe that they are its staunchest supporters are in reality fostering that form of constitutional observance which abides by the letter but violates the spirit. Is it not far better consciously to face the fact that the precedents cited are precedents in form rather than in substance? A precedent is "a decision precisely, exactly or directly, in point,"† or a case, of which the "facts cannot be distinguished in effect from those of the present case."‡ Judged by these standards can the proposition for a moment be seriously entertained that real legal precedents exist for the constitutional questions involved in the government of the Philippines; at all events as regards the applicability of the constitutional restrictions and the constitutional guarantees? In every one of the cases cited the question before the court has been, whether the benefits of the constitutional guarantees, together with the common law system which they include, should be extended to territory contiguous to the territory of the states, settled by a people of essentially the same training and traditions. Is it not natural that with expediency and traditional policy in harmony, the Supreme Court should have followed the line of least resistance?

But now the question has arisen under totally different conditions. With a population on a lower plane of civilization, untrained to the common law—in fact, in many cases devoid of any legal system—are we blindly to follow rules of interpretation intended for essentially different application? The mere statement of the possibility is a

* 76 Howard, 164 (193).
† 6 East, 512, Ram. "On Legal Judgment,"p. 113.
‡ 3 Barn. and Ald. 56.

reflection on our political capacity as a nation. When we bear in mind the splendid traditions of forbearance and self-restraint of the judiciary, the constant desire which it has shown to remove rather than to increase the obstacles to efficient government, there is, it appears to me, but little danger that we will be forced to the unpleasant choice between inefficient government and irresponsible rule.

Militarism and Democracy.

Annual Address.

MILITARISM AND DEMOCRACY.

The Annual Address, by the Honorable Carl Schurz.

The subject of "Militarism and Democracy," which has been assigned to me for discussion, is at the present moment of peculiar interest. We are apt to speak boastfully of the progressive civilization characterizing this age. While the very foundation of all civilization consists in the dispensation of justice by peaceable methods between nations as well as individuals, instead of the rule of brute force, it is a singular fact that at the close of this much-vaunted nineteenth century we behold the nations of the world vying with each other in increasing their armaments on land and sea, exhausting all the resources of inventive genius and spending the treasure produced by human labor with unprecedented lavishness to develop means of destruction for the defence of their possessions, or the satisfaction of national ambitions, or the settlement of international differences, on a scale never before known.

Thus the very advances in the sciences and the arts which constitute one part of our modern civilization are pressed into the service of efforts to perfect the engineries of death, devastation and oppression, which are to make brute force in our days more and more terrible and destructive, and to render the weak more and more helpless as against the strong. It looks as if the most civilized powers, although constantly speaking of peace, were preparing for a gigantic killing-and-demolishing match such as the most barbarous ages have hardly ever witnessed, and this at the expense of incalculable sacrifice to their peoples.

Nothing could in this respect be more instructive and pathetic than the appeal in behalf of peace and disarmament addressed last year by the Czar of Russia to all the powers represented at his court. Of that appeal this is the principal part:

"In the course of the last twenty years the longings for a general appeasement have grown especially pronounced in the consciences of civilized nations. The preservation of peace has been put forward as the object of international policy; it is in its name that great states have concluded between themselves powerful alliances; it is the better to guarantee peace that they have developed in proportions hitherto unprecedented their military forces and still continue to increase them without shrinking from any sacrifice.

"All these efforts, nevertheless, have not yet been able to bring about the beneficent results of the desired pacification. The financial charges following an upward march strike at the public prosperity at its very source.

"The intellectual and physical strength of the nations, labor and capital, are for the major part diverted from their natural application, and unproductively consumed. Hundreds of millions are devoted to acquiring terrible engines of destruction, which, though to-day regarded as the last word of science, are destined to-morrow to lose all value in consequence of some fresh discovery in the same field.

"National culture, economic progress, and the production of wealth are either paralyzed or checked in their development. Moreover, in proportion as the armaments of each power increase, so do they less and less fulfill the object which the governments have set before themselves.

"The economic crises, due in great part to the system of armaments *à outrance*, and the continual danger which lies in this massing of war material, are transforming the armed peace of our days into a crushing burden, which the peoples have more and more difficulty in bearing. It appears evident, then, that if this state of things were prolonged it would inevitably lead to the very cataclysm which it is desired to avert, and the horrors of which make every thinking man shudder in advance."

There has been much discussion as to the motives which may have impelled the Czar to make this appeal. Many of those who consider him sincere, call the manifesto a mere outburst of generous sentimentality which, although laudable in itself, loses sight of existing conditions and of the practical exigencies of the moment. If it really was mere generous sentimentality, it was sentimentality of that sort which in the history of mankind has not seldom served to give impulse and inspiration to great movements of progress in justice and humanity, overcoming with its optimism that dreary and pusillanimous wisdom which reasons that existing evils cannot be rectified simply because they are strongly intrenched in existing conditions. If it was that sentimentalism, it did honor to the Czar's heart, and, inasmuch as it attacks a terrible evil which eventually *must* be remedied, it did no discredit to the Czar's head.

Others have questioned the Czar's sincerity and good faith, suggesting that the peace manifesto was merely a diplomatic stratagem designed to dupe his competitors for territorial conquest. This is, in view of the solemnity of the Czar's words, so atrocious an imputation that only hardened cynicism will readily accept it. It is, however, all the more to be deplored that the Czar, at the time when the belief of the world in the sincerity of his benevolent purposes is so important, should himself endanger that belief by ruthlessly suppressing the constitutional rights and liberties of the good people of Finland, which he had solemnly sworn to maintain, and which his predecessors, even so stern a despot as Nicholas I. had faithfully respected. The performance of two acts so different in character by the same person may be explained on the hypothesis, that in the one case the Czar, being sincerely alarmed by what he himself experienced of the evils and dangers of excessive armaments, could not resist the impulse of attacking them, and did so in good faith, while ordinarily, in doing the business of an autocrat, he may be no better, and in some respects even worse, than others engaged in the same trade.

But however that may be, and whatever results the peace conference meeting in response to the Czar's appeal may immediately bring forth, the most important point is that the statements of fact contained in the Czar's manifesto are true. They are indeed not new. The same things have often been said before. But those who said them were promptly and derisively cried down as visionary dreamers who had no conception of the responsibilities involved in the management of the great business of the world. Now those things are authoritatively proclaimed by the most absolute monarch commanding the largest army on earth, and holding in his hand the destinies of one of the greatest empires—the man whose immediate responsibilities in the management of the great business of the world are not exceeded by those of any other human being.

While the so-called practical men of the age never cease to tell us that the greatest possible security of peace depends upon the greatest possible preparation for war, that autocrat and commander of millions of soldiers tells them that the nations which are draining their own vitality to preserve peace by their preparations for war, are doing a thing which, if prolonged, "will inevitably lead to the very cataclysm which it is desired to avert, and the horrors of which make every thinking man shudder in advance." Thus it is no longer merely the idle and irresponsible dreamer but the practical potentate charged with the farthest-reaching powers and the highest responsibilities who warns the world that if the policy of increasing armaments, which we call militarism, be persisted in, it must produce ruinous mischief, and end in incalculable disaster and calamity.

The comparative weight with which militarism, that is the system which makes the maintenance of great armaments one of the principal objects of the state, burdens different nations, depends upon their respective wealth, the length of the terms of military service, their administrative organization, and the nature of their political institutions. Upon nations which are unable to bear heavy loads of taxation, or whose finances are in a precarious state, or which suffer from official incapacity or corruption in their administrative organization, or which withdraw their young men for long periods of time from productive employments without offering through the military service any valuable compensation by way of instruction or training, the burden of great standing armaments weighs of course more heavily than upon nations whose material resources are great, or which can easily raise ample revenues, or whose administrative machinery is honest and efficient, or whose terms of military service are short, or whose young men receive in that service at least some discipline, instruction and training calculated to increase their working capacity in productive pursuits, and thus to compensate in some measure for their temporary withdrawal from such occupations.

For the purposes of this discourse the workings of militarism in France are of especial interest, on account of the political institutions of that country.

In a monarchy a standing armed force is a thing congruous with the nature of the government, and it is the more so, the more the monarchy is of the absolute type. The standing army in such a monarchy may be said to be the enlarged bodyguard of the monarch. The monarch represents an authority not springing from the periodically expressed consent of the people, and relying for the maintenance of that authority, if occasion requires, upon the employment of force, even against the popular will. An army is an organization of men subject to the command of a superior will, the origin or the purpose of which it is assumed to have no right to question. The standing army is in this sense, therefore, according to its nature and spirit an essentially monarchical institution.

But France is a republic. She calls herself a democratic republic. A democratic republic is, or should be, government by public opinion as expressed in legal form—public opinion, as it issues from discussion in which all the people are free to participate, and the outcome of which they are to determine by their freely given suffrages. The army, inasmuch as it is in all things subject to the will of superior authority without discussion or question, must therefore be regarded as an incongruous element in a democracy. The authority to which it is subject, may indeed be a government created by public opinion and supported by it. But as such a government may happen to become faithless to its origin, or fall out of accord with the public opinion of the time, the army, as an organized force subject to its will, may be used by it for ends and purposes adverse to the interests or the will of the people.

It is for reasons like this that the true democratic spirit has always been jealously opposed to the maintenance of large standing armies. It has always insisted that the organizations of armed forces that may be necessary for the enforcement of the laws and the keeping of order at home, or for the defence of the integrity or the honor of the state in foreign warfare, should remain as much as possible identified with the people themselves—should be, in fact, *of* the people in their origin, their interests, their sympathies, as well as in the character and aspirations of those commanding them; and that, if a standing army as a permanent institution be indeed indispensable for certain necessary objects, it should, in point of numerical strength, be confined to the narrowest practicable limits.

That democratic spirit has therefore always demanded that the armed force should be composed principally of the militia, the citizen soldiery,—or, in extraordinary emergencies, of volunteers called out from the ranks of the people, to serve as soldiers for certain well-defined and stated purposes, and then, those stated purposes being accomplished, to return to their civic pursuits. So it has hitherto been with us. In Switzerland, where the democratic spirit is much alive, but where on account of the geographical situation of the country a large and well-drilled force is thought necessary, they have organized the whole male population capable of bearing arms in military bodies, some of which are called out for instruction and drill for a limited period every year, to be restored to civil life after the shortest possible interruption of their ordinary occupations—the only thing resembling a standing army being certain small staff corps which are kept in permanent service. All this rests upon the leading principle that the soldiers of a democracy as well as those commanding them should, while temporarily submitting to military discipline, remain in all essential respects active citizens without any interests, or sympathies, or aspirations in any manner or degree different from those of the general citizenship.

France furnishes the example of a republic maintaining a large standing force, and the history of that country is peculiarly instructive as to the relations between standing armies and democracies. The first French Republic sprang from the great revolution of 1789. The most famous of French armies were organized under the inspiration of the revolutionary enthusiasms of that period. They were then to a large extent composed of volunteers who had rushed to arms to defend the territory of the republic, and then went forth to bring "Liberty" to the world outside. Thus they won victory, and glory, and conquest. And then, having gone forth to fight for liberty, they proceeded, intoxicated with glory and conquest, to turn their victories for liberty to the advantage of a personal government animated with insatiable despotic ambitions. I am far from saying that the spirit of the army was the only cause for the downfall of the democratic republic. But it is a matter of history that the army, which had been created for the service of democracy, was, by the glory and the conquests it achieved, transformed into a willing and most effective instrument of usurpation and tyranny at home, and of oppression abroad. And it may be said that the Napoleonic system of government which was thus created, was the beginning of that militarism with which Europe is now afflicted.

The second French republic sprang from the revolution of 1848. It was the prestige of the name of Napoleon, the glamour of the Napoleonic legend of military glory, that made the election of Louis Napoleon to the presidency of the republic possible. Usurpation followed. I do not pretend that the spirit of the standing army alone caused the transformation of the second French republic into the second French empire. But it can certainly not be denied, that the army again lent itself as a willing tool to the schemes of the conspirators who had planned the destruction of the republic, and the erection of a monarchical government upon its ruins.

After the disastrous collapse of imperial rule in the Franco-German war, the third French republic was proclaimed in 1870. It has now lasted well-nigh twenty-nine years. But the greatest dangers that have threatened its existence came from the position in it of the standing army. One of its chiefs, MacMahon, while president of the republic, was drawn into the intrigues of the monarchist parties; another, Boulanger, plotted revolution and usurpation, probably for his own benefit; and now, in these latter days, in consequence of the hideous Dreyfus affair, the administration of justice has, in the interest of the chiefs of the army, been subjected to a perversion calculated to undermine the very foundations of legal government, and, it is to be feared, ultimately to effect the total subversion of republican institutions. The domineering spirit of the army is such that it claims to be above discussion and criticism, assumes to dictate the decisions of judicial tribunals, and actually seeks to substitute for what in other countries is the crime of lèse-majesté, the crime of lèse-armée. At any rate, whatever the future may bring, it is no exaggeration to say, that the attitude of the army in France has dealt the reputation of republican government a staggering blow, and that all this may turn out to be only a prelude to new usurpations.

It is idle to pretend that all the historical facts I have enumerated, were owing only to the proverbial inconstancy of the French temperament; for it should not be forgotten that even in England, when the parliamentary forces during the so-called Great Rebellion of the seventeenth century had assumed the character of a standing army, that army, in spite of its origin, became in the hands of Oliver Cromwell a ready instrument for the transformation of the republic into a personal government essentially monarchical, and finally, under the leadership of Monk, served to bring about the restoration of the monarchy with all its forms and attributes by the return of the Stuarts. Thus we see that it was not a mere French peculiarity which made a strong standing army a danger to republican institutions in Europe, but that the large standing army has always played the same part in European republics, regardless of race. I need not go into the history of the republics of antiquity, modern instances being sufficiently instructive.

As I remarked, militarism on a great scale began in Europe with the French revolution and attained a high degree of development under the first Napoleon. It declined somewhat under the influence of the reaction which was caused by the general state of exhaustion after the Napoleonic wars. It revived again after the revolutionary movements of 1848 when the new French Emperor sought to fortify his throne by warlike prestige, when Italy and Germany moved for the accomplishment and maintenance of national unity, when continental powers, following the example of England, became ambitious of colonial expansion, and when new inventions in the appliances of warfare stimulated the powers in a course of nervous rivalry. It is thus that the deplorable conditions came about which are so pointedly set forth in the peace manifesto of the Russian Czar; that millions of young men at the period of their greatest vigor are withdrawn from productive pursuits; that "the intellectual and physical strength of the nations, labor and capital, are largely diverted from their natural application and unproductively employed" in gigantic preparations for possible conflicts of arms, and that the nations are burdened with very onerous taxes for the purpose of providing engines of destruction.

For the burdens European nations are thus bearing, the advocates or apologists of the system have a ready plea of justification. It is that the nation refusing to bear those burdens would soon be at the mercy of its ambitious and possibly hostile rivals. The Frenchman tells us that, aside from his desire to take revenge for the defeats suffered in the German war, France must strain every nerve in preparation for a possible conflict, to be reasonably secure against German aggression or British encroachment. The German reasons that, the German Empire being wedged in between France and Russia, whose sentimental alliance may on occasion be turned to hostile purposes, the fatherland must be armed to the teeth according to the latest fashion, in order to maintain the integrity of the empire, and that it must also have a strong fleet to hold its own in the race for colonial power. The Russian insists that unless his country be provided with bigger armies and navies, British, and possibly also German jealousy will become dangerous to its vital interests. The Englishman maintains that Britain must have a fleet superior to those of any probable combination against her, and also a strong fighting force on land to protect the safety of her isle and of her widespread possessions against the ill-will of other nations which would be likely to avail itself of any favorable opportunity to strike at her with effect.

And thus no sooner has one of those nations taken the slightest step to increase the numerical strength of its armaments or their efficiency in killing and destroying; no sooner has it begun to augment its battalions, or squadrons, or batteries; no sooner has it introduced a new model of musket or of cannon; no sooner has it built a warship upon a new plan promising to do better execution, than all the others with nervous anxiety will follow suit or even try to push a step further ahead. And this process must be gone through again and again, whole armies must be newly armed, and whole fleets must be rebuilt, as the crack ships of yesterday have become little better than old iron to-day. And all this, no matter what burden be put upon the backs of the people, nor how the taxpayer may groan. In fact, those governments claim that they are not permitted under these circumstances to adapt their policy concerning their armaments to what may be their own wishes, or to what they might consider good for the welfare of their people. Their necessities in this respect are determined, not by themselves, but by the performances of their neighbors and rivals. And so the ruinous competition goes on and on without end in sight, the moloch of militarism being insatiable.

A striking example of this race of competition was recently furnished in England by the First Lord of the Admiralty, Mr. Goshen, when he asked the House of Commons to appropriate the enormous sum of £26,554,000 ($132,770,000) for the British navy, saying that so startling an estimate had not originally been contemplated, but that it had been framed after a careful study of the programs of the other powers; that the United States, Russia, France, Japan, Italy and Germany had under construction 685,000 tons of warships, and that England was compelled to shape her action accordingly. He prayed that, "if the Czar's hopes for disarmament were not realized, those who proposed to attack the country's expenditures would not attempt to dissuade the people from bearing the taxation necessary to carry on the duties of the empire."

In France the minister of war not long ago dolefully intimated that he apprehended France had reached the end of her possibilities, not having men enough to match the increases of the much more populous German Empire. As a member of a republican government he might have said more. He might have added that a large standing army makes a monarchy more monarchical, but that it makes a democracy not more, but less democratic; that the more absolute a monarchy is, the more a large standing army will fit it, but that the more democratic a republic is, the less a large standing army will be suitable to it; that to a monarchy it may be a standing support, but that to a democracy it will be a standing danger.

So far the American people have been exempt from most

of the evils springing from this system. From the foundation of the government it has been the consistent policy of this republic, following the true democratic instinct, to adapt its armaments to its own needs, without permitting itself to be drawn into the vortex of rivalry with other nations. As to the maintenance of peace and order at home, it has ordinarily depended upon the local police forces and the militia. It kept a small standing army stationed at a few military depots, a few coast defence fortifications, or at posts in the Indian country. It kept a small navy just sufficient for an occasional showing of the flag in foreign waters and for doing its part of the police of the seas. Whenever an extraordinary emergency arose, such as a war with a foreign power, or an insurrection of formidable proportions at home, it organized armed forces on a larger scale by calling out volunteers who were enlisted in the service of the republic, not as a regular standing army is, for doing whatever task might turn up, but for a well-defined, specific purpose, to be disbanded again as soon as that specific purpose was accomplished.

So it was held on the notable occasions of the war of 1812, of our war with Mexico, and of our great civil war. And I venture to say that no nation ever presented to the world a grander, more characteristic and more inspiring spectacle than this republic did when, after the close of the civil war, hundreds of thousands of men who had been organized in great armies, as soon as their task was done, quietly dropped their guns and as good citizens went home to devote themselves to the productive work of the country—the vast armies disappearing as by magic. It was a grand spectacle, I say, grander in its way than the most splendid victories those armies had achieved. That this republic, against the misgivings entertained abroad even by our friends, proved such a thing to be possible without the slightest difficulty, was one of the finest lessons ever taught by a great democracy to mankind.

Such was our normal policy during the period between the

foundation of the republic and our days. Times of war excepted, the republic was, compared with other nations, substantially unarmed, and, considering the condition of our coast fortifications, substantially defenceless. And yet it cannot be said that, since the war of 1812, it was, in consequence of its unarmed state, at any time in serious danger of foreign aggression or of a serious denial of its rights by any foreign power. Not as if all foreign nations had been our sworn friends, eager to keep us from harm in our innocence —for there were people enough in Europe, and even in America, who disliked us and would not have been sorry to see this republic perish;—nor as if in our intercourse with foreign nations we had been over-anxious to spare other people's feelings—for the tone of our diplomacy was not always a model of politeness. No, it was because in the main we took little interest in matters which did not concern us, and because every foreign power understood that, considering our vast resources, and the compactness and substantial impregnability of our great continental stronghold, a serious conflict with the United States would mean to our antagonist a test of endurance which no European power could undergo without offering seductive opportunities to its rivals or enemies in the old world, and that therefore it was wise to avoid so hazardous an embroilment at almost any cost. This feeling became especially distinct in Europe after the unexpected display of strength the United States made in the civil war, and after the equally unexpected reconciliation between the North and the South so soon after the close of the conflict.

The American people were therefore perfectly right in their sense of security while in an unarmed condition. There was really no danger to threaten us, unless we ourselves provoked it. Even the warning which we heard now and then among ourselves, that our foreign commerce would not be safe without being protected by a larger war fleet, was groundless. For it is a matter of history that even before those demonstrations of our strength in the civil war, when we had with our sailing ships a very large part of the carrying trade of the world, without any navy worth speaking of for its protection, our foreign commerce proved as safe as that of any other nation having ever so many guns afloat. In fact, ever since the war of 1812, we have not had a single difference with any European power that could not be settled on fair terms without our having any ready armament to enforce our will. The proof of this is in the historical fact that they were so settled. It is a matter of speculation whether they would all have been settled so peaceably if we had possessed an armed force ready and itching for a fray.

Thus the policy of this republic was in entire harmony with that democratic instinct which abhors large standing armaments, and our position among the nations of the world was singularly favorable to the maintenance of that policy. None of those anxieties arising from the possible hostility of powerful neighbors, which keep European nations in a heavily armed state, existed here. Absolutely nothing to alarm us. Neither was there any reason for apprehending that those happy conditions would change, unless we ourselves desired to change them. There has indeed, of late been much talk about the necessity of enlarging the field of our foreign commerce, and of increased armaments and even of the acquisition of foreign territory to sustain our commercial interests in foreign quarters. But while that talk was going on, our commerce was very extensively enlarging its foreign fields without big fleets and without colonies, by its own peaceful action. We simply produced, in our factories as well as on our farms, more things that other nations wanted, and we could offer them at prices with which other nations could not compete. This golden key of industrial progress and peaceful commercial methods opened to our trade many doors which seemed to be closed against it by all sorts of artificial obstructions; and this peaceful expansion of our foreign commerce went steadily on while other nations that had an overabundance of battalions, batteries and warships, vainly struggled to keep pace with it. These are facts, undenied and undeniable.

But what will happen to us, commercially, if other nations seek by force to monopolize certain fields of trade for themselves, and in the course of that effort come to blows with one another? Then a sober and circumspect calculation of the advantages to be gained, and of the price they would cost, will probably lead to the conclusion that in such a case a strong neutral power would enjoy very favorable opportunities and in the end have the best of the bargain. And when I speak of a strong neutral power, I do not mean a neutral power so fully armed that it might at once successfully cope with any of the belligerents, but I mean a neutral power strong enough in its resources and in its position to make each belligerent extremely anxious to abstain from anything that might drive it to the other side. Such a neutral power this republic was not in its infant state during the Napoleonic wars preceding our war of 1812, when both belligerents, France as well as England, thought they could kick and cuff this republic with impunity; but such a strong neutral power this republic, with its seventy-five millions of people and its immense wealth, would be now. No belligerent would dare to disregard its neutral rights; and at the end of the fight, the combatants well exhausted, it would probably be in a fair position to exercise a very powerful influence upon the terms of settlement.

Such a policy, harmonizing with our principles as well as our traditions, safe as well as advantageous, would not oblige us to keep up large and costly armaments; and it would at the same time teach our business men to rely for profit, not upon benefits to be gained for them by force of arms, subject to the fortunes of war, but upon their own sagacity in discovering opportunities, and their own energy in using them—which in the long run will prove to be after all the only sound basis of a nation's commerce under any circumstances.

There seems to be, then, in all these respects not only no necessity, but no valid reason for our turning away from the old democratic policy and embarking in that course the pursuit of which costs European nations so dearly, and which they justify only on the ground that the constantly threatening dangers of their situation actually force them to follow it. On the contrary there would seem to be overwhelming reason for doing everything to preserve our happy exemption from such dangers and necessities, as a blessing so exceptionally great that the American people could not be too grateful for it.

But we are told that there are certain populations in distant lands to whom it is our duty to carry the blessings of liberty and civilization, and that this may require larger armies and more warships. However laudable such a purpose may be, if sincere, it behooves us as sensible men soberly to consider the consequences of the attempt. I have already spoken of the armies of revolutionary France, that went forth to fight for general liberty, and that conquered for despotism. It cannot be denied that those French armies brought to some of the peoples they overran certain beneficial reforms. But with those reforms they brought foreign rule, and most of the "liberated" peoples found foreign rule more hateful than they found the reforms beneficial; and they availed themselves of the first favorable opportunity to throw off the foreign rule of the "liberators" with great slaughter.

We may flatter ourselves that, as conquerors, we are animated with purposes much more unselfish, and we may wonder why not only in the Philippines, but even among the people of Porto Rico and of Cuba, our benevolent intentions should meet with so much sullen disfavor. The reason is simple. We bring to those populations the intended benefits in the shape of foreign rule; and of all inflictions foreign rule is to them the most odious, as under similar circumstances it would be to us. We have already seen in the Philippines the beginning—for it is a mere beginning—of the resistance to foreign rule by one of our "liberated" peoples—a bloody game far from exhilarating. We may expect by a vigorous application of our superior killing power to beat and disperse Aguinaldo's army; but it is by no means unlikely that more insurrections against foreign rule will follow. They may be suppressed, too, but the surviving spirit of them will oblige us to keep much stronger forces on the ground than we ever anticipated, in constant apprehension of further mischief. Our rule will continue to be foreign rule then with the smell of blood on it.

Nor is it by any means impossible that the vulnerable spots thus added to our dominions—a point of weakness we so far have never had—may encourage some jealous and unfriendly foreign powers to take advantage of our embarrassments and to involve us in broils which so far we never had any reason to dread. Or the apparent necessity to protect what conquest we have made, by further conquests, or the ardor of military or naval commanders a little too anxious to serve their country with their guns, may plunge us into the most hazardous complications. Of the chances to which we shall thus be exposed in many places, the utterly absurd Samoan affair furnishes an illustration. We may assume that the greatness of our resources will enable us to issue victorious from such conflicts too. But it will not be denied—in fact, it is already conceded—that persistence in such a course will oblige us very materially to enlarge our standing armaments, and subject us more and more to those burdens which what is called "militarism" is imposing upon the groaning nations of the old world. Patriotism as well as ordinary prudence, demands us to consider what those burdens are likely to be.

In 1897 our standing army consisted of 27,500 officers and men. The appropriations for the support of that army amounted for that fiscal year, to $23,278,000, which sum did not include expenditures for fortifications. The average cost of each man in the army was therefore about $850. It is generally admitted that if we continue the so-called new policy, we shall need a standing army of certainly not less than 100,000 men—probably more, perhaps a good many more. I do not pretend that the average annual cost of a soldier will under all circumstances rise or fall with the size of the army. But it will not be questioned that such average cost will be much higher when the troops are used in distant places beyond seas, especially in tropical climates, where the soldiers have to endure very unfavorable sanitary conditions. Even if there be little or no active campaigning to be done, it is certainly a moderate assumption that the service of a large part of the army beyond seas in tropical regions would raise the average cost of a soldier to $1,000 a year. This would make an army of 100,000 men cost at least $100,000,000, or over $76,000,000 more than our army cost before the Spanish war. But if active campaigning is to be done, if the "mowing down" of "insurgents," fighting for their freedom and independence, lasts long and has to be carried on during the sickly season, the replenishing of the depleted ranks, the feeding of the troops, the maintenance of an effective hospital service, the restoration of destroyed war material, the transportation of reinforcements to the theatre of operations, and of the wounded or sick back to the home country, and all the multifarious things incidental to warlike action even on a small scale, would cause expenditures beyond the possibility of accurate computation.

We are not a very economical people. We are apt to become lavish and wasteful upon the slightest provocation. Even a little war will cost us much. Whether the little war with Spain, which was practically over in three months, has cost us less or more than $500,000,000 may still be a matter of doubt. I speak here only of the cost in money. The cost in blood and misery I leave you to think of.

That, if the new policy be persisted in, our naval establishment also will have to be much enlarged, is generally admitted. How much—who can tell? Certainly, *we* can *not* tell. For it will not depend upon us how many new battleships, and armored or unarmored cruisers, and light draft vessels, and torpedo boats, and destroyers, we shall want. It will depend upon the naval armaments our rivals and possible enemies have on the field of competition. Until recently, when we were proud, not of possessing large armaments, but of not needing any, it has afforded us much occasion for compassionate amusement to observe the almost hysterical nervousness into which old world governments were thrown when one of them began the building of new warships by which the proportion of power on the seas might be disturbed. Already we begin to feel that nervousness in our bones, and we cannot tell how many and what kind of warships we shall be obliged to have in order to maintain what is so vauntingly called our new position among the powers of the world.

Nor will any amount of new construction set the matter at rest for any certain time. We do not know when we shall have to rebuild the larger part of our fleet; for, as the Czar truthfully says in his manifesto, "the terrible engines of destruction which are to-day regarded as the last word of science, are destined to-morrow to lose all value by some new discovery in the same field." All forecasts as to the expenditures for naval purposes which the new policy will impose upon us in the course of time, are, therefore, futile. But whatever they may be, the people will have to pay the bills.

Moreover, we have to bear a burden of which other nations know comparatively little. During the last fiscal year we paid over $140,000,000 in pensions. More than one hundred years after the revolutionary war, more than eighty years after the war of 1812—for we still have some widows of soldiers in those wars on our pension rolls—fifty years after the Mexican war, and thirty-three years after the civil war the number of pensioners was about one million. And still they come. It is estimated that the recent Spanish war will add $20,000,000 to our annual pension expenditure. It will probably be much more. The pension attorneys and members of Congress looking for the soldier-vote will take care of that. But if we continue the military occupation of tropical countries there will be a constant stream of new pensioners owing to tropical diseases; and if we have any active military operations in those tropical regions, that stream will be heavy beyond calculation. And it will be without any end in sight. We must therefore look for a considerable increase of the pension charge for an incalculable period—the number of new pensioners overbalancing the number of those who in the natural course of things may be expected to drop out—that dropping out being notoriously very slow. Our annual pension expenditure now exceeds the whole cost of the great German army on the peace footing, its pension roll included. As our pension charge threatens to become, it may approach for a time the annual cost of the whole peace establishments of the empire of Germany and the kingdom of Italy combined.

Taking it all in all, assuming our standing army not to exceed 100,000 men, but a large part of it to be engaged in the tropics, and our navy to be gradually enlarged to the strength which it "must have" in order to enable this republic to play the part of a colonial power, we are sure to have, including our pension roll, an annual expenditure for army and navy purposes not only far exceeding that of any European power, but not falling very much short of two-fifths of the expenses for the same purposes of all the six great powers of Europe together—that is not far from $400,-000,000 a year. By honest and strenuous effort we have paid off the bulk of the heavy national debt left by the civil war, and we have been very proud of that achievement. We are now in the way of running up a new national debt, of which, if we go on with the new policy, nobody can foretell to what figures it will rise.

It may be said that the American people, owing to their large and ever increasing numbers and to their extraordinary resources will be much more capable than other nations, of bearing such taxation, and therefore feel it less. That is true. But it is also true that it will yet be a painful burden upon the labor of the people, and contribute neither to their well-being nor to their contentment unless the burden, as well as the resulting benefit, be equitably distributed. To justify heavy taxes for military purposes beyond absolute necessity we should, therefore, economically speaking, show two things: (1) that the benefit derived from the employment of the money raised by such taxation will exceed the value of the money thus taken out of the pockets of the people; and (2) that such benefit will accrue to the several taxpayers, or classes of taxpayers, in substantially just proportion to their respective contributions for the purpose in view.

Thus it would in our case be necessary to prove: (1) that if we increase our taxation so many hundred millions a year for the purpose of enlarging our standing armaments to the end of establishing and maintaining our rule in the West Indies and the Philippines, the profits from the expansion of our business enterprise accomplished thereby would exceed that amount—a matter about which, to say the least, there is extremely grave doubt; and (2) that such profits from whatever increase of business there may be, will directly or indirectly redound in substantially just proportion to the people who pay the taxes—in other words that, while the taxes to sustain our foreign enterprises are levied upon the great mass of the people, the poor as well as the rich, they will redound really to the general benefit of the people, and not merely, or mainly, to the profit of a comparatively small number of capitalists who are able to take advantage, in a more or less speculative way, of the chances that may offer themselves in those distant regions. About this, too, there is exceeding grave doubt.

These are points which I have no time to elaborate here in detail; but I commend them for serious consideration to good citizens who are disposed to look before they leap; for they involve not only an economic question, but also one of justice.

Let me now pass to the institutional aspect of the case as it concerns this republic in particular. I am far from predicting that the organization and maintenance and use of large armaments will speedily bring forth in this country the same consequences which they did produce in England in Cromwell's time, and in France at the periods of the first and the second French republics. With us the "man on horseback" is not in sight. There is no danger of monarchical usurpation by a victorious general—although it is well worthy of remembrance that even here in the United States of America, at the close of the revolutionary war, at the very threshold of our history as a republic, a large part of the revolutionary army, "turned by six years of war from militia into seasoned veterans," and full of that overbearing *esprit de corps* characteristic of standing armies, urged George Washington to make himself a dictator, a monarch; that, as one of his biographers expresses it, ' it was as easy for Washington to have grasped supreme power then, as it would have been for Cæsar to have taken the crown from Antony upon the Lupercal;" and that it was only George Washington's patriotic loyalty and magnificent manhood that stamped out the plot. However, usurpation of so gross a character would now be rendered infinitely more difficult, not only by the republican spirit and habits of the people, but also by our federative organization dividing so large an expanse of country into a multitude of self-governing states.

But even in such a country and among such a people it *is* possible to demoralize the constitutional system and to infuse a dangerous element of arbitrary power into the government without making it a monarchy in form and name. One of the most necessary conservative agencies in a democratic republic is general respect for constitutional principles, and faithful observance of constitutional forms; and nothing is more apt to undermine that respect and to foster disregard of those forms than warlike excitements, which at the same time give to the armed forces an importance and a prestige which they otherwise would not possess.

No candid observer of current events will deny that even to-day the spirit of the new policy awakened by the victories and conquests achieved in the Spanish war, and by the occurrences in the Philippines, has moved even otherwise sober-minded persons to speak of the constitutional limitations of governmental power with a levity which a year ago would have provoked serious alarm and stern rebuke. We are loudly told by the advocates of the new policy that the constitution no longer fits our present conditions and aspirations as a great and active world power, and should not be permitted to stand in our way. Those who say so forget that it is still our constitution; that while it exists, its provisions as interpreted by our highest judicial tribunal are binding upon our actions as well as upon our consciences; that they will be binding and must be observed until they are changed in the manner prescribed by the constitution itself for its amendment; and that if any power not granted by the constitution is exercised by the government or any branch of it, on the ground that the constitution ought to be changed in order to fit new conditions, or on any other ground, usurpation in the line of arbitrary government is already an accomplished fact. And if such usurpations be submitted to by the people, that acquiescence will become an incentive to further usurpations which may end in the complete wreck of constitutional government.

Such usurpations are most apt to be acquiesced in when, in time of war, they appeal to popular feeling in the name of military necessity, or of the honor of the flag, or of national glory. In a democracy acting through universal suffrage, and being the government of public opinion informed and inspired by discussion, every influence is unhealthy that prevents men from calm reasoning. And nothing is more calculated to do that than martial excitements which stir the blood. We are told that war will lift up people to a higher and nobler patriotic devotion, inspire them with a spirit of heroic self-sacrifice, and bring their finest impulses and qualities into action. This it will, in a large measure, if the people feel that the war is a necessary or a just one. But even then its effects upon the political as well as the moral sense are confusing. When the fortunes of war are unfavorable, almost everything that can restore them will be called legitimate, whether it be in harmony with sound principle or not. When the fortunes of war are favorable, the glory of victory goes far to justify, or at least to excuse, whatever may have been done to achieve that victory, or whatever may be done to secure or increase its fruits.

History shows that military glory is the most unwholesome food that democracies can feed upon. War withdraws, more than anything else, the popular attention from those problems and interests which are, in the long run, of the greatest consequence. It produces a strange moral and political color-blindness. It creates false ideals of patriotism and civic virtue.

Nobody is inclined to underestimate the value of military valor. But compared with military valor, we are apt to underestimate the value of other kinds of valor, which are equally great and no less, sometimes even more, useful to the community. I do not refer only to such heroism as that of the fireman, or the member of the life-saving service on the coast, who rescues human beings from the flames or from the watery grave at the most desperate risk of his own life, and whose deeds are all the more heroic as they are not inspired by the enthusiasm of battle, and pale into insignificance by the side of any act of bravery done in killing enemies in the field. I speak also of that moral courage more important in a democracy, which defies the popular outcry in maintaining what it believes right, and in opposing what it thinks wrong.

Blood spilled for it on the battlefield is often taken to sanctify and to entitle to popular support any cause, however questionable. It is called treason to denounce such a cause, be it ever so bad. It is called patriotism to support it, however strongly conscience may revolt against it. Take for instance the man who honestly believes our war against the

Filipinos to be unjust. If that man, faithfully obeying the voice of his conscience, frankly denounces that war, and thereby risks the public station he may occupy, or the friendship of his neighbors, and resolutely meets the clamor vilifying him as a craven recreant and an enemy to the republic, he is, morally, surely no less a hero than the soldier who at the word of command and in the excitement of battle, rushes against a hostile battery. You can no doubt find in our country an abundance of men who would stand bravely under a hailstorm of bullets. But many of them, if their consciences condemned the Filipino war ever so severely, would be loath to face the charge of want of patriotism assailing everybody who opposes it. This is no new story. War makes military heroes, but it makes also civic cowards. No wonder that war has always proved so dangerous to the vitality of democracies; for a democracy needs to keep it alive above all things the civic virtues, which war so easily demoralizes.

You will have observed that I have treated the matter of militarism in the United States in intimate connection with our warlike enterprises, as if they were substantially the same thing. I have done so purposely. As I endeavored to set forth, the development of militarism in European states can be explained on the theory that each power may think the largest possible armaments necessary for the protection of its safety among its neighbors, and for the preservation of peace. With us such a motive cannot exist. Not needing large armaments for our safety—for this republic, if it maintained its old traditional policy, would be perfectly safe without them—we can need them only in the service of warlike adventure undertaken at our own pleasure, for whatever purpose. And here I may remark, by the way, that in my opinion, although such a course of warlike adventure may have begun with a desire to liberate and civilize certain foreign populations, it will be likely to develop itself, unless soon checked, into a downright and reckless policy of conquest with all the "criminal aggression" and savagery such a policy implies. At any rate, that policy of warlike adventure and militarism will, with us, go together as essentially identical. Without the policy of warlike adventure large standing armaments would, with us, have no excuse and would not be tolerated. If we continue that policy, militarism with its characteristic evils will be inevitable. If we wish to escape those evils and to protect this democracy against their dangerous effects, the policy of warlike adventure must be given up, for the two things are inseparable.

I have referred to the current events of the day only by way of illustration, without giving full voice to the feelings which they stir up in my heart, and the utterance of which might be somewhat warmer than what I have said. My theme being the relation of militarism to democracy in general, and to this great American democracy in particular, I may be permitted to express, in conclusion, my views of what our policy as a democracy should be in order to keep the vitality of the democratic republic unimpaired.

We should, in the first place, restrict our standing armaments to the narrowest practicable limits; and those limits will be very narrow, if this democracy does not suffer itself to be carried away by the ambition of doing things which, as history has amply shown, a democracy cannot do without seriously endangering its vital principles and institutions. There is no doubt that a regular standing army is a more efficient fighting machine, especially at the beginning of a war, than citizen soldiery. But our experience has been that, in the peculiar position we occupy among the nations of the world, we need not have any war unless, without any compelling necessity, we choose to have it. It would be most unwise to shape our whole policy with a view to the constant imminence of war, there being no such imminence, unless we ourselves choose to create it. We should have as our main armed force, and as the natural armed force of a democratic republic, the citizen soldiery to be called out for specific purposes in extraordinary emergencies, the efficiency of that citizen soldiery to be increased by the training of men to serve as officers, and by the organization of staff corps, upon a plan similar to that adopted in Switzerland. We should have a navy strong enough to do our share in the police of the seas, but not a navy rivaling those of the great naval powers, for, as our history has conclusively taught us, we shall not need it if we keep out of quarrels which do not concern us, and cultivate peace and good will with other nations—a disposition which the rest of the world will be glad to reciprocate. In this way we shall avoid the burdens and evil influences of militarism, and give even our pension roll at last a chance to decrease.

Following a policy essentially different from this we may have our fill of military glory and conquest, but with them, other things which in the course of time will make the American people ruefully remember how free and great and happy they once were with less military glory and with no outlying dominions and subject populations.

The Commercial Relations of the United States with the Far East.

Addresses and Discussions.

THE COMMERCIAL RELATIONS OF THE UNITED STATES WITH THE FAR EAST.

WORTHINGTON CHAUNCEY FORD, *Ex-Chief Bureau of Statistics U. S. Treasury Department.*

If "prophecy is a gratuitous form of lying," it is almost inexcusable when undertaken in a period of great change and transition. Two continents are being partitioned among the nations of Europe, a partition that cannot but influence the world's movement for a century to come. In Africa the larger part of the task stands completed. Boundaries and spheres of influence have been fixed so far as they can be by treaties and arrangements based upon a common or mutual interest. There is yet some room for changes, but only at one point—Delagoa Bay—can the result be of great moment. In Asia the work is just beginning, and there is every opportunity for greed, intrigue, moral influence, humanity, every passion that a nation can endure to defend its safety, to accomplish its policy, or to gratify its selfishness.

Examine the coast of China as it was only a few years ago. France had won Tonking and Indo China. Portugal held Macao, a place of no naval strength, because so overshadowed by the English island of Hong Kong. Its advantage lay in its being near the mouth of one of the great rivers of China, the only river of the south penetrating to the inner provinces. From Hong Kong to Korea no part of the coast was subject to foreign control. In Korea Russia and Japan were about to fight their contest diplomatically, and the Russian eventually to win. The break came with the Sino-Japanese war. Russia obtained the right to bring its great railroad down to Port Arthur, and began to exercise a preponderating influence in Chinese councils.

This menace of Russian control over an empire that had just been shown to be weak beyond description, aroused in other nations a desire to share in the spoils. Germany, under the plea of defending its missionaries and merchants, obtained under threats a lease of the great peninsula of Shantung. Great Britain, by diplomacy, and we know what is back of such diplomacy, leased sufficient territory on the mainland above Hong Kong to render that station safe from any land attack. France obtains a lease of Lei-chau on the promontory at the southern end of Kwang-tung. In the next province—Fo-kien—the Japanese are claiming the right rather than the privilege of establishing themselves. Moving northward, we next meet the Italian claims, involving a lease of the bay of San-mun and three islands off the coast. At the next stage occurs the English sphere in the Yang-tze valley, one that will hardly be surrendered, so high are its value and possibilities held. By the side of the Germans in the Shan-tung peninsula are the British at Wei-hai-wei, a great naval base. Belgium comes forward to ask a concession at Han-kau, whereon to construct the Lu-ban railroad. In this way the entire coast of China is held under one form of control or another, by foreign nations, not one of whom has any interest in maintaining the integrity of the empire, unless such maintenance can prevent rivals from securing more than a fair share of the spoil.

This is certainly a remarkable position for any people to occupy. No charge is made against the Chinese, such as could lie against the followers of the Mahdi, of being a menace to civilization. It can not be said that the Chinese neglect their opportunities as did the Turk, or are hopeless economically, as were the Indians of America, the natives of Africa, or the aborigines of Australia. On the contrary the more that is known of China and the Chinese, the greater is our wonder that in such a mass of population, weighted down by poverty, conservatism and hatred of progress in any form, so much is done, and well done. They have not merited extermination, our brutal exclusion laws to the contrary; and wherever they have gone, and they move freely, the testimony is universal, that as laborers only, they are willing, industrious, patient and efficient. To have their coast occupied by foreign squatters, not one of whom would not resent a similar move on their own territory, and to be bullied and badgered into giving valuable concessions and privileges which have gain for their object, whatever may be the good intentions of the parties—surely this is a sight to awaken a doubt as to the actuating motives.

Into this circle of marauding powers the United States was pitched unexpectedly and without any thought of the consequences. Being in the Philippines, by purchase, and about to occupy them by conquest over the natives, the fact must be accepted. The ruling motive for accepting the responsibility was commercial; given those islands, it was said, our trade with Asia must be large. They can be used as a stepping stone to secure entrance to the continent, and our farmers or manufacturers, or shipping interests and our Congress will feel a quickening influence, and awake to better things. It is the commercial aspect I wish to dwell upon, and this involves our trade with all Asia.

In 1898 15 per cent of the total imports into the United States was derived from Asia, and 3.63 per cent of the exports were sent to that continent. In 1889 the percentages were 8.55 for imports and 2.48 for exports. In the earlier year the aggregate value of imports was $63,600,391 and in 1898, it was $92,594,593—an increase of 45.6 per cent. The value of the exports (domestic) rose in the same period from $18,422,922 to $44,642,613 an increase of 142.5 per cent. The whole of this increase in exports has occurred since 1895.

The distribution of this trade is necessary to a proper understanding of the growth. Imports from China have been stationary, but exports have ranged between wide limits, depending on the movement of cotton cloth:

Year.	Imports.	Domestic Exports.	Cotton Cloths.	Mineral Oil, Refined.
1889	$17,028,412	$2,790,621	$1,519,265	$908,500
1890	16,260,471	2,943,790	1,223,965	1,253,089
1891	19,321,850	8,700,318	5,334,860	2,591,660
1892	20,488,291	5,663,471	3,887,732	1,251,025
1893	20,636,535	3,900,457	1,638,657	1,809,437
1894	17,135,028	5,858,488	2,844,220	2,438,636
1895	20,545,829	3,602,741	1,703,023	1,181,210
1896	22,023,004	6,921,136	3,854,146	2,166,978
1897	20,403,862	11,916,888	7,438,203	3,371,973
1898	20,326,436	9,992,070	5,195,845	2,839,345
Total		$62,289,980	$34,639,916	$19,811,853

Second in importance comes Japan, which is even now regarded as the prototype of what China will be when once awakened. Imports from and exports to Japan prove the remarkable activity of that country in building up its foreign commerce:

Year.	Imports.	Domestic Exports.	Raw Cotton.	Mineral Oil, Refined.
1889	$16,687,992	$4,615,712	$2,341	$3,086,978
1890	21,103,324	5,227,186	85,211	3,573,798
1891	19,309,198	4,800,650	223,879	2,894,577
1892	23,790,202	3,288,282	132,729	1,812,414
1893	27,454,220	3,189,711	68,423	1,724,972
1894	19,426,522	3,981,377	360,492	2,226,247
1895	23,695,957	4,559,242	806,058	1,656,692
1896	25,537,038	7,640,250	1,481,056	3,149,527
1897	24,009,756	13,233,970	2,345,016	4,222,383
1898	25,223,610	20,354,689	7,428,226	3,592,587
Total		$70,891,069	$13,133,431	$27,940,175

The great distributing centre of Asiatic trade, Hong Kong, has not held its own in the commerce of the United States, and has suffered through more direct means of communication. Its share in our trade is so small as to be inappreciable, though in our trade with Asia it still receives $6,233,607 of our exports, and handles $746,517 of merchandise sent to this country. In any calculation of the trend of our trade with Asia, Hong Kong may be passed over in the statistics, but examined for its lessons.

Other than independent (I still apply the adjective to China) countries are counted in the Asiatic returns—the colonial possessions of Great Britain and the Netherlands, and even Aden and Turkey in Asia. But it is to China and Japan that I wish to call particular attention, and if I deal at greater length with China, it is because so much stress is laid upon our future commerce within rather than with that empire. On that future must the prosperity of the Philippines rest; and on that future hang our relations to Europe —entangling alliances imposed upon us by commercial ambition.

Let us measure crudely the export trade of the United States to China. For the ten years, 1889–98, the value of our domestic exports sent to that empire was $62,289,980, of which 87 per cent was made up by two articles of export —cotton cloths and refined mineral oil. In 1889 the proportion of the exports for that year given by these articles was 87 per cent; in 1893, five years later, 88 per cent, and in 1898, another interval of five years, 80 per cent. Up to 1898, it was 87 per cent and over, almost without a break.

Taking the exports to Japan in the same manner, it is found that the total for the ten years was $70,891,069, and of this total raw cotton made $13,133,431, and refined mineral oil $27,940,175, or the two, 58 per cent of the whole. Of the increase in the exports since 1889 ($15,738,977) raw cotton gave nearly one-half ($7,425,985). The stationary character of the trade in one country and the elasticity of the demand in the other could hardly be more clearly or simply demonstrated than by these figures. In 1889 raw cotton did not enter appreciably in the export returns to Japan; in 1898, it made more than 36 per cent.

China is poor and not rich. One of the latest and in many respects most intelligent surveys of China says: "There is in China a dreadful poverty of the masses due to rapid increase of population, wherever a district has been spared rebellion and famine for a few tens of years."* The vast population is never far removed from famine, and only by constant industry of the most exacting kind can life be sustained. Large numbers of Chinese flock to other lands to obtain a living. They have swarmed down the Malay Peninsula, crossed to the Philippines and attempted to gain a foothold in Australia. They are numerous in the Hawaiian Islands, and have secured the hostile notice of both the United States and the Dominion of Canada. The Chinaman is the laborer for the world, and carries his patient and persistent industry wherever permitted, and his frugal habits enable him to save from wages that no other free laborer would accept. The coolie is a privileged worker compared to him.

Wherever tested and an opportunity given, the Chinaman has proved himself a good worker. The problem then to be settled is how this hive of potential industry can be made to work on the natural resources of China for the benefit of the nations of the West. No one denies the possibilities of Asia; its coal fields, its iron, its tin and its copper deposits; its wonderful waterways, and its population that always seems to offer a market rich beyond description. Against this rosy picture must be set the poverty of the people; their conservatism and hatred of the foreigner; and their decay of enterprise, a decay that has persisted in spite of the touch of Western commerce, and the lesson of defeat at the hands of the Japanese. Now Europe steps in to realize the possibilities, and offers to lead and organize the economic forces of China, so that they may become truly productive and yield handsome dividends to these unselfish civilizers and concessionnaires.

If this development occurs the whole world expects to share in the benefits, and the United States will ask to have its share. But in one direction, more than in another; in imports, rather than exports. In opening new territory by

* Blackburn Report (Bourne), 10.

making it accessible, and thus giving to the population an outlet for their products, the world's supply of certain articles will be that much increased. Tea, silk, raw cotton, wool, hides, mats and straw braids—these are the great articles of China's export trade with occidentals, and in these lines must the first influence of new conditions be felt. Later will come the greater changes which portend almost to revolutionize industry—the opening and working of coal mines, of iron, copper, tin and even gold deposits, mineral resources hardly touched and known to be large. Given an abundance of cheap labor, a certain and cheap transportation to the coast, and the old sources of supply must feel the influence of these new rivals. If the raw materials are worked on the spot or in the coast cities, great industrial enterprises run without regard to the cost of life—the cheapest product in China—it is possible to picture the condition apprehended by Pearson, the overrunning of Europe and America with the products of the yellow races. Each nation will strive to secure the utmost gain, for combinations will hardly be possible, and production will attain a great pitch of quantity and of lowness of price.

In place of hiring and transporting coolies to distant plantations, this labor will be available on the spot; and instead of being an import of value, the very plenty will make it cheap; while care and protection will cause it to increase. Exports will thus be without hindrance.

How about the imports? In this question the United States has a lasting interest, and a great uncertainty. Of the imports into China, cotton goods hold the first place, opium the second, rice the third, and metal manufactures and mineral oil are of equal importance, as fourth and fifth on the list. In no one item of this enumeration has the United States a natural monopoly; in only one (petroleum) has it a partial monopoly, fast being impaired; and in two (rice and opium) it has and can have no share. Even assuming that China remains as she is, and the ports held by Europe, a cordon of duties would check any growth of our exports whether from the United States or the Philippines. The English territory will probably be free, though it is by no means certain that with duties on all sides, her manufacturers will not demand some assurance of the markets they are taxed to maintain and defend. Elsewhere our products will meet with discriminating tariffs designed to secure the cream of the trade for the mother country. Where will the increase in our export trade be sought?

But China will not remain as she is. France, Germany, Italy, England, Russia—these nations have gone to Asia for a purpose. They intend to build railroads, open and develop mines, establish industries, and secure all they can from a careful attention to encouraging competition on Asiatic conditions. In place of wanting cottons, products of iron and steel, or other metals, or rice, China will utilize her own resources. This may be a work of time, but under the stimulus of so many competitors it will not require many years to bring it to pass. Every ton of iron, of copper or of tin wrought into metal ware in China; every pound of wool or of cotton, or of silk made into cloth in the provinces, will reduce the necessity of importing them from other countries.

A mere comparison of commercial details develops the distinction between Japan and China—a living and pushing people and a decayed and dying empire. In Japan opium does not stand prominent in the import returns, but the leading place is taken by raw cotton. Second in place is sugar, the consumption of which is by some regarded as a gauge of civilization. Textile and metal manufactures form a large item, and the imports of machinery have increased more than sevenfold in ten years. Not raising sufficient food for its people, it is from other countries that the necessary grains must be obtained. The ability to buy of foreign nations has increased from $29,700,000 in 1886 to $94,800,000 in 1896, and the purchases have all been in needed or useful commodities.

To pay for these imports some domestic products were called for, and herein the organizing ability of the Japanese came into play. Tea and silk were the two important articles of export, the same that China sent into the world's commerce. The problem then presented was how a larger share in the existing market for these commodities could be obtained, and a share in any increase of market offered. China, by neglect of reasonable precautions, suffered the quality of both her tea and silk to degenerate, and the outside buyers were not slow to determine this fact. The value of teas exported from China has hardly varied in the last thirteen years, nor has raw silk followed another course. Only in silk cocoons and in manufactured piece goods of silk (including pongees) has there been an increased export. Japan, on the other hand, paid great attention to her products, and has reaped her reward. The exports of silk have doubled since 1885, and those of silk manufactures have risen from less than 270,000 yen in 1885 to 16,232,000 yen in 1895, and have attracted hostile duties in both France and the United States. The movement of tea has not been so progressive, showing only a small increase; but coal has quadrupled (2,004,000 yen in 1885, and 9,018,000 yen in 1896) due to Indian competition; cotton manufactures have gone from 181,000 yen in 1885 to 3,378,000 yen in 1896; manufactures of wood, bamboos, etc., from 112,000 yen to 6,129,000 yen; and of copper (raw) from 8,183,000 catties to 11,241,000 catties. In the aggregate, the exports have increased from $31,630,000 in 1885 to $61,571,000 in 1896.

Many have seen in this advance a picture in small of what will occur in China on a grand scale. There are certain differences that may be noted. The character of the two peoples are different, and the Japanese have much higher organizing powers. "The truth is that a man of good physical and intellectual qualities, regarded merely as an economical factor, is turned out cheaper by the Chinese than by any other race; he is deficient in the higher moral qualities, individual trustworthiness, public spirit, sense of duty and active courage, a group of qualities perhaps best represented in our language by the word manliness; but in the humbler moral qualities of patience, mental and physical, and perseverance in labor, he is unrivaled. . . .

"European superintendence is essential precisely because of their moral shortcomings above stated. Judged by our standards, we must pronounce all organizations in China (with a few exceptions) above the family and the small business partnership, to be hopeless failure. The upper class seem to lack the moral tone to carry on by enterprises; indeed the laws and the courts of justice are wanting as well as the men."*

Japan fearlessly went into the money markets and obtained the capital needed for her enterprises. China is held under a crushing weight of custom, of stagnating civilization, and is to be in tutelage for the account and profit of others. No one can doubt for a moment that Europe does not regard the coast provinces as the end of their leases or cessions, or occupations. It is the great interior of China they have in view, and are so anxious to develop. The claim of Italy may be taken as a sample. A lease of the bay, and three islands in it—these matters are first; then the right to build a railroad to Po-yan Lake about one hundred and fifty miles from the sea is claimed, a claim that extends to running the railroad after construction. This is important, as many rivers empty into this lake, navigable into the interior of the surrounding country. Finally preferential mining and railroad rights within a sphere of influence covering two-thirds of the province of Che-kiang—a province containing 36,000 square miles (about one-third as much as Italy herself) and a population estimated at 20,000,000 (about two-thirds the present population of Italy). So France in Tonking has her eye on Yunnan, and England, at the mouth of the Yang-tze, hungers for the trade of provinces 1,500 miles from that mouth, but only to be reached through it at present. Germany and Russia are no more neglectful of the prospective virtues of hinterlands. A map colored to meet the wishes of these land grabbers would resemble that of the

*Blackburn Report (Bourne), 9.

American colonies of England, when charters were granted to extend from the Atlantic Coast to the South Sea. So anxious are they to obtain a part of what is lying waste that combinations are made like the Anglo-German negotiations for a railway from Tien-tsin to Chin-kiang; and the railroad enterprise over which England and Russia have nearly come to blows.

There are certain obstacles which stand in the path of the commercial development of China, and these obstacles now effect the merchants and products of all nations trading with the Chinese, though not in an equal degree. There is the natural disadvantage of the want of roads and easy access to the interior provinces. There are the rivers, to be sure, and they are great waterways. Apart from them the system of porters is used, a slow, painful and somewhat costly process of transportation. For many commodities it is prohibitive, and it practically confines the export interests of the far western provinces to such products as are of small bulk, and high value—silk and opium. The mountainous regions have mere tracks rather than roads, so narrow that the shoulder poles cannot be used; and a light frame strapped on the back of the coolie takes its place. "The weight which a coolie can carry in this way is perfectly astonishing, and it is a common sight to see him struggling over the most execrable roads having on his back three bundles of Sha-si made cloth, each containing thirty-nine pieces, equal to a load of 220 pounds. Of cotton yarn the load is 160 pounds, and one frequently meets coolies carrying 160 pounds of tin or copper, which has come from the mines in the district of the Tung-chuan."* Pack animals are not generally used, a coolie can carry a larger load, and while he takes a longer time is quite as cheap—3*s*. 2*d*. being a charge for 130 miles.

The first change must be toward constructing better roads where water carriage is not available. Cochin China and Tonking are favored by their many water courses, both

* Blackburn Report, Neville and Bell, 78.

rivers and canals. Not only do these favor the cultivation of rice, but permit a ready shipment of the crop, just as Virginia and North Carolina were favored in their rice and tobacco days by the same means of getting direct to the plantations. Annam and Cambodia are wanting in rivers. The West River of China is not available to trade; but the Red River promises a means for the French to reach Yunnan —called "the natural economic complement to Indo-China." Even the further sections of the Yang-tze offer serious problems to the navigator—rapids and a rise of seventy feet during the freshets. The Yellow River is more uncertain in its course than our Mississippi, and it is a common occurrence for it to leave its bed, plow a new course through a densely populated country, carrying death and destruction in its new path, and leaving drought and famine in its old. Railroads will supplement river traffic but can never supersede it; and for some time railroad ventures will be costly, uncertain and experimental.

Good means of transport and communication will avail little without a thorough revision of the tax question. This means a reform of provincial or local administration. The likin on imports and the duties on exports not only limit the distribution and consumption of foreign products, but place China at a disadvantage with rival peoples. The existence of these taxes is an encouragement to official corruption, and it is estimated that of every three taels collected, only one reaches the imperial treasury. The burdens imposed by a series of likin barriers, each one taking its toll at a rate fixed by the local authority, involve serious loss and discouragement to trade. Hong Kong is the natural port for the southern provinces. But the impositions levied on merchandise on the West River make it more profitable to take goods intended for Kwang-si to the seaport of Pakhoi, thence partly by boats and partly by porters to the upper waters of the West River, a journey of eight days. One reason for resorting to coolies is the desire to avoid likin stations.

The likin question has in a measure determined the position

of the foreign merchant in China. Generally speaking it has been the treaties with foreign countries that fixed the rights and privileges of the foreigner on Chinese territory. But a subtler and even more powerful influence has neutralized the advantages expected to flow from treaty provisions, and a change of some moment has been wrought so quietly and yet with such determination, that the foreigner, as merchant, may be said to be out of China.

What has been the position of a merchant in China until a very recent time? He possessed a bare right to import and export at certain ports established by treaty. In these ports he occupied a "concession," that is a piece of ground leased by the Chinese Government to his own government, and sublet to the merchant; or a "settlement," an area within which he may lease land directly from the native authorities. He could not manufacture, he could not mine or engage in agriculture. He was a mere commission merchant, for outside of these places, the internal trade is in the hands of the Chinese, "excellent peddlers" as they are. Of late some concessions have been made. By treaty privilege steamers may be sent up the Yang-tze to Ch'ung-king, a distance of 1,400 miles from the sea. Under the treaty of Shimonoseki the right to manufacture has been granted and machinery may be imported. Twenty-one ports are treaty or open ports.*

It was the purpose of the negotiator of the treaty of Tientsin to lighten some of the burden of these likin or local charges, and the transit pass system was the outcome. On payment of the legal customs duty at the port of entry, and one-half that tariff in addition, goods, whether import or export, should be free to pass between the port of shipment or entry, to or from any part of China, without further charge of toll, octroi, or tax of any description whatsoever.†

* These are : New Chwang, Tient-sin, Chefoo, on the northern coast; Chung-king, I-Chang, Shasi, Hankow, Kiu-kiang, Wuhu, Chinkiang, and Shanghai, on the Yang-tze River, Ningpo, Wenchow, Foochow, Amoy, Swatow, Canton, Hoihow (Kiungchow), and Pakhoi, on the coast south of the Yang-tze; and Hang-chow and Soo-chow, two cities in the neighborhood of Shanghai.
† Lord Elgin, in China No. 4, 1870.

In practice the intentions of the pioneers of the system have been neutralized, and in some places to such an extent as to make an "open port" an illusion.

At Wuchow, for instance, the privilege is evaded by imposing differential duties on transit pass goods. Or the transit passes are recognized only while the commodities they cover are in foreign hands; as soon as they reach Chinese merchants, the demand for likin is made. Or the pass is accepted and at the end of the journey a "terminal" charge is imposed. Taxation is made the easier because it is imposed on the Chinese merchant.

One result of this system is to crowd out the foreign merchant, in both the import and the export trades. It has been the impression that the opening of a new port in China to commerce involved a concession to foreigners. In practice it has been found it is the native merchant who benefits. The carriage of any article in vessels of a foreign type, or even in native craft in which foreigners may claim to have an interest, at once withdraws those commodities from the control of the native customs with their petty exactions and unscrupulous charges. "At the present day, to open a new port to foreign trade may mean little else than giving to native merchants at that port the blessing of a fixed tariff and an honest customs administration."—*Brenan, 54.*

"The impression which a visit to nearly all the treaty ports of China leaves upon the mind is that the Chinese people are monopolizing in an increasing degree the commercial advantages obtained under the several treaties which foreign governments have concluded with China. Foreign powers having prepared the ground for their nationals, the Chinaman is gradually elbowing them out and occupying the position for himself."[*] Chiefly at Hong Kong and Shanghai is the British merchant found. In most of the ports it is the Chinaman, and he is becoming the more important commercial factor. Not only does he buy of the

---

[*] Report of H. B. M. Consul Byron Brenan, on the State of Trade at the Treaty Ports of China, 1896.

agent at Shanghai or Hong Kong, but his orders are given for imports to be made. Of the textiles imported from Europe and the United States, it is estimated that one-half is specially indented for under instructions from Chinese dealers. Cotton and woolen goods apart, seventy-five per cent of the other imports at Shanghai is on Chinese account. The foreign firm, through whom the order has been given has no interest in the goods on arrival, beyond their security for the payment by the Chinese principal. It is a commission transaction, not that of a merchant.

This situation is not favorable to the expansion of China's commerce. Every advantage secured by foreigners has been obtained by treaty, and often by a treaty extorted under a threat or actual exertion of force. Every privilege secured by treaty is intended to make commercial intercourse more free and more possible. The foreign merchant under cover of the treaty may do many things without interference from the authorities, but the Chinese merchant would be subject to that interference.

While the foreign merchant may plead treaty rights, and generally secure them, the native merchant is powerless. He has no government to back his complaints, he can hope for no aid from agitation, for the simple reason that he dare not agitate. As soon as he begins to move his goods into the interior he meets the likin, and at many stages of his journey. The officials could wreak a disastrous vengeance upon him should he incur their displeasure, and he has no redress against their extortion. Illegal taxation and vexatious detention of goods already exist; they may be so intensified as to throttle trade. Hence the disadvantage of distributing through Chinese merchants.

Export trade from China is in foreign hands. "A change is noticeable. Where years ago a few large firms with large capital bought China's products and sent them to Europe on their own account, there are now many small firms who receive orders from Europe by telegraph, and who fulfill these for a small commission at no risk to themselves. The telegraph and banking facilities have made it unnecessary to possess capital, and the business of the export merchant in China has in a great measure changed into that of the commission agent. One of the consequences of this is that the commission agent who is buying on a limit, and who receives a commission on the amount of the invoice, buys on the best terms he can at the treaty port, but has no personal interest in the previous treatment which the merchandise has experienced at the hands of the tax collector, and does not feel disposed to engage in the interminable disputes which an attempt to profit by the treaty stipulations affecting the inland transit of merchandise would land him in. Were he dealing with his own money, and was every dollar saved in taxes a dollar in his own pocket, he probably would try to bring his taxation down to a legal minimum; but in filling an order he now takes what the local market offers, and makes no research into the past."—*Brenan, 14, 15.*

Hampered as it is by local dues on both imports and exports, dues which even the ingenuity of native merchants cannot evade, the special products of China are placed at a disadvantage in foreign markets. Silk is taxed in the cocoon, before it can pass into the hands of a foreigner; and tea lands pay a growers' tax that cannot be evaded by transit passes. This disadvantage alone will not explain the fact that the Asiatic trade is more or less confined to Asiatic countries. China's total imports in 1886 were 89,310,000 Hk. taels, of which 59,497,000 taels—or two-thirds—were from Asiatic countries. In 1896, the same percentage held, two-thirds of a total of 211,623,000 Hk. taels (140,408,000 taels) being of Asiatic origin. But only 41 per cent of China's exports in 1886 were sent to Asiatic countries, and 64 per cent in 1896.* Japan's commerce gave almost the same result. In the two years, 1886 and 1896, about 30 per cent of the total imports was Asiatic; but 23 per cent of the exports in 1886 went to Asia, and 32 per cent in 1896, as follows:

* Total export in 1886, 77,207,000 Hk. taels; to Asia, 31,893,000. In 1896, total, 131,081,000 Hk. taels; to Asia, 83,657,000 taels.

1886, total import, 37,637,000 yen; from Asia, 11,348,000 yen.

1896, total import, 188,666,000 yen; from Asia, 60,122,000 yen.

1886, total export, 48,871,000 yen; to Asia, 11,273,000 yen.

1896, total export, 129,455,000 yen; to Asia, 41,954,000 yen.

The trade of British India is pertinent on this point. The exports of merchandise and treasure by sea were returned at £90,113,171 in 1887, and £108,840,187 in 1897—an increase of 20 per cent. The exports to all Europe rose from £56,610,000 in 1887 to £58,450,000 in 1897—an increase of only 3 per cent; while those to Asiatic countries were £24,507,112 in 1887 and £33,849,257 in 1897—an increase of nearly 40 per cent. The development of Indian export interests has wholly been toward Asia. In imports the showing is better for Europe, for the trade of that continent to India increased in ten years at nearly the same rate as the trade of Asia to India—21 per cent for Asia and 22 per cent for Europe. It is with Egypt, Japan and Russia and Asia that the largest returns of increased imports are shown.

This has been in a measure the experience of Great Britain with British India. In 1897, the year of latest returns, the total exports of India by land and sea were £113,400,000, of less than one-third (£34,786,000, or 30 per cent) was sent to the United Kingdom. Standing between two continents, with such a facility as the Suez canal to favor the trade with Europe, India sells to that continent £58,405,000 or a shade over one-half of its total export movement. This may be taken as an unusually favorable showing for the argument in favor of commercial expansion, but the United States in 1898 sent 80 per cent of its exports to Europe, and counting in what was sent to North American countries, the proportion rises to 90 per cent. Second in importance among the colonies feeding the trade of the United Kingdom is Australasia, with its varied interests and products. Excluding gold, the total exports in 1897 were £65,350,000, of which £26,000,000—nearly 40 per cent—was sent to the United Kingdom. Turning to the English trade returns it is seen that the total imports from Australasia were £29,352,000, of which £16,785,000— 57 per cent—was in wool, a concentration of import interest that is in itself remarkable. If we add a single item from four of these dependencies, butter from Victoria (£816,400); tallow from New South Wales (£661,000); fresh beef from Queensland (£725,000), and fresh mutton from New Zealand (£2,077,000), 72 per cent of the entire imports from Australasia into the United Kingdom is accounted for.

Returning to purely Asiatic colonies of Great Britain the Straits Settlements exports £18,000,000 a year, but only one-seventh goes to the United Kingdom, and if all Europe be included, less than one-fourth is sent direct. Mauritius sends only £45,000 of a total of £2,846,000 to the United Kingdom, and the demand of all Europe for its products (of which sugar is the great one) will not double that amount. Ceylon is more devoted to English interests, for two-thirds of its exports are taken by the United Kingdom, due to the peculiar product of tea. If a very few articles are excluded from the export trade of these Eastern possessions—tin, tea, jute, hides and skins and wool—what remains has little attractions for Europe, and is Asiatic in availability.

The Netherlands holds important islands in the East, and their trade is naturally largely with the mother country through fiscal arrangements. It is a trade resting on an artificial basis, but now passing through a transition stage, and a difficult one to foresee in its results. The leading products for export are sugar, coffee and tobacco. The sugar crop is experiencing the same pressure as throughout the world; the cultivation of coffee is passing more and more into the hands of individuals, and the production of tea, tin, cinchona bark, indigo and tobacco points out the future lines of growth for the island

Being more and more Asiatic in its export character, how can some of the benefits of Asia fall to the United States?

Only in two ways, it is said: by establishing Manila as a free port; or by manufacturing for Asia on an Asiatic basis.

Make Manila a free port, it is said, and the United States will be in a position to claim its share in Asia's trade. How can this be? The example in mind is clearly Hong Kong, but the history of that island shows how it was favored by conditions not likely to be repeated. The striking fact about Hong Kong is that it was not China but the Chinese that made it possible and have made it what it is. For a long time it was a morgue spot: "the White Man's Grave," and an Alsatia, a place of refuge for the lawless or criminal, and its future was in doubt as late as 1848. Then came a series of events: the discovery of gold in Australia and California made the coolie trade profitable; the Taiping rebellion which drove men of property to the island for protection; the Suez canal and its effect on Eastern commerce; and the opportunities for work offered in the Malay Peninsula. From a struggling town no better than a mining camp in morals, it has become one of the great shipping centres of the world. "In the colony of Hong Kong," says Colquhoun, "most of the wealth is in the hands of the Chinese, and in all the chief business houses and financial institutions the Chinese hold positions of great responsibility."* For some years the commerce of Europe at Hong Kong has shown a tendency to decrease, a fact that can be explained only by the change in the direction of Asiatic commerce, by which the transactions are more and more among the peoples of Asia and less with the countries of Europe and America. Further, the over-sea commerce tends to become more direct, and the need of a port of deposit or for transshipments is less felt.

Nor geographically can it be said Manila offers any advantage to Asia's trade. There is already a great shipping station at Singapore, for the Indian commerce, and it is quite as convenient to steam from Singapore to Hong Kong, as it

*China in Transformation, 316.

would be to go to Manila and thence to Hong Kong, or any port of Asia. If the advantage of a free port is not to be had, the only alternative is to use the Philippines as a manufacturing base, for supplying the continent with certain manufactures, like low grade cotton cloths. Native labor, if available, and native cotton would be used, after the manner proposed by the French in Tonking. In that event the question of labor would again come to the front. Would an attempt be made to use the natives, or to bring coolies from China? The success of either would be problematical, against the establishment of mills in China itself.

As an agricultural colony the Philippines have their possibilities, for there is a natural monopoly in Manila hemp, and a capacity for all tropical growths. But the labor for the plantations, where is that to be had? Spain used the natives, but only under a system that ruined the planter and drove the laborer into rebellion. The methods purported to be in imitation of those adopted by the Dutch in Java. "The [Spanish] law prescribed that every native might plant tobacco, but might only sell it to the government. In the tobacco districts every native had to grow a certain number of plants and devote all his attention to them." Here all similarity ended. The tobacco was sorted by the officials and the unfit burned. "For valuing the tobacco the officials used a scale, according to which the planter received some 20 to 30 per cent of the real value. But he was not paid in cash. He received a certificate, a kind of treasury bond. Had the people had security for the payment of these bonds at an early date, the latter would soon, no doubt, have come into currency as paper money. But, far from this being so, no one would have them, knowing that five or six years might pass before they were redeemed. The tobacco planters lived under more miserable conditions than the worse kept slaves, and were glad if some noble philanthropist would give them half the value of their certificates, for who could say whether the purchaser was not risking his 50 per cent. Frequently the bonds were practically given away."*

Tobacco, hemp and sugar, these are the three leading products of the island, and all paid export duties under the Spanish rule. The tobacco finds no market in the United States; the sugar will be at a disadvantage with the Cuban and Hawaiian products, and must a find market in China; and hemp can not find an indefinitely increasing demand. There are minerals. The coal is of a quality that unfits it for transportation and must confine it to local use. Gold is reported, and copper is known to exist. Iron ore is abundant, but the lignites of the archipelago are said to be unsuitable for blast furnaces, and charcoal pig is the method suggested.† The copper deposits were worked for a time, but were abandoned for want of labor. It is too sanguine a view to accept Mr. Tornow's view: "It is certain that the Philippines, whose future is already assured by their mineral wealth, will play a part in the industry of the coming years equal to, if not surpassing, that of Japan." Even if we accept his view it leads us to the conclusion that the commerce must be for Asia, not for the United States.

Another straw indicating the direction of trade winds. When Japan obtained possession of Formosa, a tariff of ten per cent ad valorem on imports went into operation. This increase, applying as it did to all imports from foreign countries fell as much on Chinese as on British cottons. Some compensation was expected from the privilege of free circulation of goods throughout the island. In the event Japanese and Chinese cloths have excluded all grades of foreign cloth coming in competition, leaving a much restricted demand for finer grades to be satisfied by Great Britain.

In Japan there are a million spindles now in operation, producing, 650,000 bales of cotton yarn of 400 lbs. each, of which more than 200,000 bales will be sent to China. In the needs of no other textile industry in Japan can the United States have

*Tornow, "The Philippine Islands."
† George F. Becker of the U. S. Geological Survey.

a share either in the raw material or manufactured product. Silk is out of the question, wool is obtained from Australia and China, while woolens are cheaper in France, Germany or Great Britain than here. Flax and hemp are to be had from the Philippines, China and British India. Is it too much to look for an imitation of Russia's policy, which has sought to make that country independent of our fibre by developing the culture in Asia?

Is not this Asiatic commerce beset by a new difficulty offering a new problem of no little moment? Every port of size on the coast is in the hands or under the control of some European nation. We have set an example by declaring the Philippines open for ten years, and Mr. Reid assures us they will never be closed. What assurance have we that Continental Europe will maintain open ports in Asia? France in Tonking has been exclusive, and her coming policy is foreshadowed by her measures taken in Madagascar within a year. A decree gave a monopoly of the coasting trade to French vessels; it was promptly recalled, only because it was found the vessels flying the French flag were insufficient in number and tonnage for the needs of commerce. The application of the home tariff to the island, in itself a hardship to foreign merchants, was followed by a commercial campaign on the part of the "General Commander-in-Chief of the Corps of Occupation and the Governor-General of Madagascar and dependencies." "I have also to request you to instruct the native authorities," ran his circular, "to exert all their influence in favor of the objects at which we are aiming [to introduce French products]. It will be easy for them from the point of view now before us, to represent to persons living under their jurisdiction, that tissues of French manufacture are as good as similar articles manufactured abroad; that it is only fitting that the Malagasy, who have now become French subjects, should conform to our national customs by using our products; that their clothing thus becomes a distinctive mark of their new position, and that it should be made of

French tissues. . . But they must bear in mind that no obstacles should be placed in the way of the sale and circulation of foreign merchandise. Your part, as well as that of your native subordinates, consists simply in making clear to our new subjects the benefit to be derived by them from the purchase of French products, which will henceforward be more suitable to their habits and wants, which have been modified in the last two years by the introduction of French laws and customs. Such a course is absolutely within our right, and no one has any right to take exception to it." Further, the columns of the Malagasy journal (the *Vaovao*) were open to advertisements of French products, free of cost to the advertiser.* This found an echo in the French parliament. Introducing the debate on the colonies, March 6, 1899, M. Etienne said: "Surely France did not colonize for the benefit of foreign nations." As a result of this policy the exports of French cotton piece goods of all kinds to Madagascar rose from 690,400 francs value in 1897 to 5,512,000 francs in 1898. What reason to expect more liberal ideas in Tonking?

Another point must be considered. In order to raise the money necessary to pay the war indemnity to Japan, China mortgaged to the lenders the greater part of the receipts from customs revenue. It is generally known that the financial methods of China are not elastic, and favor a host of officials in the provinces rather than supply the imperial treasury. The land tax, which is the chief item in each provincial budget, is immutably fixed by law, and any attempt to increase it would lead to rebellion. As a monopoly the impost on salt has reached its limit, and it would be dangerous to make it heavier. Trade is, and has been the most reliable source of income, under the administration of a foreigner; but what is to happen when each port is under a different head, and competing with one another after the fashion peculiar to five rival governments? The "cohesive power of public plunder" makes itself felt under the

*Circular No. 346, printed in the *Journal Officiel*, twenty-third April, 1898.

mandarins ; but would be entirely wanting under German, French or British rule.

Here then is a cordon drawn round China, more obstructive than any Chinese wall, and liable on many accounts to be made effective as a complete prohibition on commerce. It might be assumed the privilege of trade could be assured by treaty, for a longer or shorter period. Where has a treaty been able to stand in the way of interested attack? The tripartite control of Samoa does not offer as many occasions for difference, as would the holding of the Chinese coast for commercial reasons by six great powers, and among the six the United States will not figure. The dual management of Egypt, was child's play compared to the problem of Chinese management. What has occurred in Africa, where the native counts for nothing, is only a pale forecast of what may happen in China with six nations contending for commercial advantage among a people numbering 300,000,000 souls.

Bearing in mind that the natural resources of the East are to be exploited with all the perfection of modern appliances and cheaper labor than has ever been offered, the following questions suggest themselves: How can cotton goods of the United States find other than a limited market in Asia against the cottons of India, Japan and China? How can American petroleum, better article as it is, hold more than its own against the Russian oil, supported as it may be by a bounty for political effect? Then there are the oil fields of Langkat to be counted in as competitors. How can American iron and steel enter markets held to be closed by European countries, each one of which wishes to keep for its own people the construction of the railroads, the building and running steam vessels, and the profits of the custom house? What better chance will there be for American machinery, the rolling stock of a railroad, the mining machinery and certain textile machines, than now presents itself? Finally, are we looking forward to meeting Asiatic competition with an even higher tariff than is now endured, a tariff bristling with duties like those on silks in the present law, specially leveled against the imports of light silk goods from Japan ?

THE COMMERCIAL RELATIONS OF THE UNITED STATES WITH THE FAR EAST.

ROBERT T. HILL, *U. S. Geological Survey.*

The storm centre of world interest undoubtedly now hovers over the far East and it is well that the people of this nation, while not participating in the struggle for territory, should seriously consider their interests in this distant region and how they may be protected in the field in which others are now engaged.

Mr. Ford in his address has analyzed the elements of the commercial relations of the far East and little remains to be said from the statistical point of view. He has given many of the facts concerning the actual conditions of trade and his paper is so exhaustive that he has left but little room for additional data, other than the indulgence in generalizations and conclusions.

This Eastern question has but little relation to the recent history-making events in which our nation has been engaged and should not be confused with our problems of territorial expansion. The late expansion of our nation has not been the result of governmental intent, but the culmination of great forces acting through the individual atoms of society which moved irrelevant to any preconceived political plan. Most of this growth, like that of the butterfly, has been within the cocoon, and it is only within the past year that we have emerged from the chrysalis stage into a conspicuous form which attracts the attention of the outer world and astonishes even ourselves with our own magnitude and powers. No one here can predict or judge how or where these newly felt powers will lead us. The dynamic forces of our expansion have been the superior quality of the citizen which our institutions have created, his desires for individual improvement and gain, manifested in mechanical inventions, commerce and trade, and his capacity for initiation and administration. The spirit of the United States has been to develop in every citizen the capacity for personal expansion and the growth of the nation is but a natural result of the aggregate uplifting and outspreading capacity of these units. It is the possession of these forces that gives us a feeling that we are competent to compete with the world and to meet any emergency, industrial or political, that may arise.

There are some Americans who believe that we can continue to exist entirely upon our own adipose, and who do not yet appreciate that we have become a world power, or realize that with our 5,000 miles of coast, our numerous maritime cities and our unlimited capacities for building and manning ships, we own an interest in the ocean as well as in the land. I have seen our nation pass through the most remarkable epoch of its history. My boyhood days were spent in helping reduce the vast unsettled wilderness which this country still possessed twenty-five years ago and which at that time was considered unlimited for settlement and productiveness. I have spent my later years in studying foreign regions where I was constantly impressed with opportunities for the extension of American commerce. These studies enabled me to see the approaching importance of our foreign trade and gave some definite opinions, which when expressed, resulted in securing the appellations which my conservative friends variously applied—a jingo, an expansionist and an imperialist. My jingoism, however, has consisted of a wish to see American trade stand upon an equal footing with that of all other countries; a desire for the inauguration of good government at home and the suppression of those conditions abroad which tended to prevent the flag which protects our commerce from receiving the universal respect to which it was entitled. It is my privilege to have a wide acquaintance with all classes and kinds of people in this country and I am happy to say that I do not know an American who has in his heart a desire to wrench from any other nation a foot of territory or seize unjustly that which does not belong to us. Hence the term expansionist, in so far as it applies to the principle that we should hold that which has legitimately become ours, may be considered a designation of honor. Neither do I know in this wide country of ours a single man who desires to upset our democratic institutions or to take from the people and invest in a sovereign a single one of these inestimable rights which it has been their pleasure to enjoy. Hence the term imperialist is a meaningless misnomer borrowed from English colonial politics, which have no counterpart in this country. Whatever terms may be applied to those who uphold our recent expansion in the Caribbean and the Pacific, I do not believe that any American desires to see this country participate in the acquirement of Chinese territory.

For one hundred years our people found an outlet for their energies and expansive forces in developing and conquering their own territory, in opening mines, and establishing systems of internal communication, and above all educating the youth to a degree of general mentality not approached by any other nation in the world. Suddenly we found that the nation no longer possessed undeveloped lands to bestow in exchange for the energy of those who would reclaim them; that the cream of our national resources had been garnered from public to private ownership. But the impulse of enterprise which our educational and political systems had set in action still remained with us as a force of great potentiality which is bound to be felt in foreign fields.

The events of the past year, by which our national conditions have been bettered, were not a sudden outbreak upon our part, but represented the culmination of a war which has practically continued since the beginning of our national experiences. The second page of Schouler's history describes how Spain in the very first year of our existence was a stealthy foe of the United States. The favorite saying of a captain-general of that time was that had he the power he would prevent the birds from flying across the boundary between the United States and Mexico. Since then Spanish sovereignty adjacent to our Southern border has been a source of irritation and annoyance which placed unjust and uncivilized restriction against the natural laws of trade, and prevented our commercial development in that direction. History will look upon the events of the past year merely as the equitable and righteous end of a century of irritation. The Philippine question is an unexpected incident of this war with Spain, which was primarily fought to protect our commercial relations in the Western hemisphere. These islands have come to us as the legitimate prize of a just and civilized war upon our part without preconcerted thought or desire to acquire such distant and extraterritorial domain, although their acquirement at this time gives us a timely and needed vantage which we did not before possess. Their acquisition is an entirely distinct and separate proposition from the broader Eastern question in which this country has had a deep and vital interest for many years, at least since the Chinese and Japanese ports were first opened to Western trade.

Broadly stated, the problem of our commercial relations with the far East, including under that term all of Indo-Pacific Asia, is the preservation of the present opportunities and the enlargement of future possibilities in one of the many fields of trade which make up the aggregate of our commerce. This area embraces about 10,500,000 square miles of territory, inhabited by 815,000,000 people—three times the area of the United States and twelve times the population. In its restricted sense the Eastern question applies to China only, and involves the reclamation of the Chinese people from a world retarding and inefficient culture, and their elevation into factors of greater productivity. There are other and perhaps as important fields of trade nearer home which one might well argue are more worthy of our attention, notably the commerce of our South and Central American neighbors. These are dormant fields, however, which are not threatened by cloture and will await our future attention.

The Eastern Sphere of Trade includes the following countries:

Country.	Area. Square Miles.	Population.
Borneo	290,000	1,750,000
Celebes	71,000	2,000,000
Chinese Empire	4,218,000	400,000,000
British India	1,560,000	300,000,000
Indo China	138,000	17,000,000
Java	51,000	24,000,000
Japan	148,000	40,090,000
Korea	82,000	10,000,000
Siam	300,000	5,000,000
Sumatra	161,000	3,000,000
Philippes	114,000	7,000,000
Oceanica	3,480,000	5,100,000
	10,613,000	814,940,000

When it became apparent that the powers of Europe had determined to dismember and seize upon the Empire of China, our people were naturally amazed and alarmed concerning the effect of this policy upon our own commercial relations. Sober second thought, however, must lead us to the conclusion that the effects of such a partition instead of being detrimental to our interests, will be to our advantage and prosperity. No great benefit to our trade in the East may be expected should Asia be permitted to remain Asiatic. It is only in the near possibility of its being Europeanized in commerce and government that any future gain for our trade and commerce is to be sought. I maintain that even that portion of the Chinese territory which comes under the control of those nations practicing the "closed door" policy will prove a more fertile field of trade to us than China in its present condition, for "closed doors" can sometimes be opened, while Chinese walls have no doors at all.

It has already been clearly shown how essential Caucasian superintendence is to the development of China, and no one doubts that under such superintendence the wealth producing and wealth consuming capacity of that country will be enormously multiplied. Stimulation of commerce is what this country should most desire in China, and it can but reflect great credit upon our trade just as the development of South Africa has done. The reasons for this belief are as follows:

1. China will to a degree be Caucasianized inasmuch as large and intelligent European administrative populations will be introduced whose customs and habits will be imitated by the natives. Each European wears and uses perhaps ten times as many commodities of trade as an Asiatic. Europeans to-day consume nearly eight times as much of our products as all the races of the world combined. In round numbers Europe takes $805,000,000 of our exports, Asia, $40,000,000; South America, $35,000,000; Oceanica, $20,000,000, and Africa, $15,000,000. The presence of Europeans in China will create and enlarge the markets for foreign goods. The effect of Western civilization upon Oriental life can be seen by comparison of Japanese imports with those of China.

Barbaric China Imports.	Civilized Japan Imports.
Cotton goods,	Rice,
Opium,	Pulse,
Metals,	Sugar,
Kerosene,	Chemicals,
Woolen goods,	Raw cotton,
Coal,	Cotton yarn,
Raw cotton,	Woolen yarn,
Fishery products.	Flannels,
	Muslins,
	Cloths,
	Blankets,
	Steel rails,
	Watches,
	Oil cakes,
	Spring machinery,
	Steam vessels, and a hundred other articles aggregating in value all the above.

Within the past ten years our trade with Japan, both imports and exports, has increased by annual bounds and jumps, the former having increased 50 per cent and the latter 345 per cent. This can be attributed to no other cause than the awakening of Japan through its adoption of Western civilization.

Furthermore the foreign trade with civilized Japan with a population of 33,000,000 amounts to $289,517,000, or $9.60 per capita, while the total trade of China with twelve times the population amounts to only $34,000,000, or less than nine cents per capita of population. Who can doubt that the introduction of Western civilization into China will develop an enormous foreign trade just as it has done in Japan?

We need not look with despair upon the rapid growth of the foreign trade of Japan which has doubled in eleven years. That country has allied itself in civilization and habit with England and ourselves and we should regard its prosperity as a welcome element in the otherwise dark political panorama of the East. If she has increased the number of her spindles and competed with our manufacturers of cotton goods it has had no appreciable effect upon that industry in this country, for our cotton mills, notwithstanding this competition, are enjoying the first epoch of undoubted prosperity for many years, and have apparently found market for all they can produce. Furthermore, the development of cotton manufacture in Japan has been a beneficial factor to the cotton producer of this country and already cargoes of our raw material have found new markets in that country. I have recently heard of several propositions to cultivate cotton by irrigation on the Pacific Coast of North America for the purpose of supplying the Japanese demand.

I have prepared a table showing our imports and exports with the Eastern Asiatic countries from the year 1886 to 1898, inclusive. (See page 138.)

The partition of China has been practically going on during the years included in these statistics, especially since the last Japanese war (1895). These figures show that our trade with the Eastern countries has been steadily increasing notwithstanding the constant encroachment of European occupation. Our imports from China have remained stationary, while our exports have increased 174 per cent. In all the other countries of the East our trade has in general been normal and has held its own. Furthermore, our trade with the Asiatic Russia, including Korea, has actually grown into measurable proportions from almost nothing ten years ago. The prosperity of this trade has increased proportionately with the pressure of European influence in the far East and has been especially prosperous for the past four years, our exports having increased during that time to China, the Dutch East Indies, the British East Indies, Hong Kong, Japan, Korea, and Asiatic Russia. These figures indicate the beginning of American prosperity in the East rather than the commencement of a dismal epoch of exclusion.

The stimulation resulting from the introduction of European influence into the far East has already been felt by our commerce. Mr. Ford in his statistics has shown us how much the trade of the far East has increased since the partition of China practically began with the end of the Japanese war in 1895. In 1889, 8.55 per cent of our imports came from Asia; in 1898, 15 per cent. In 1889 only 2.48 per cent of our exports went to that country; in 1898 3.63 per cent. Of this increase 46 per cent in our imports and 76 per cent in our exports took place during a single year of partition, a fact which is indeed most gratifying. This is but a fraction of what the increase will be when the political conditions of China which Mr. Ford so graphically describes, are abolished. Surely if partition has had any influence at all upon this trade it has so far been most quickening.

2. European occupation of China will abolish the unfortunate and incompetent political conditions which have been

EXPORTS FROM AND IMPORTS INTO THE UNITED STATES FROM THE FAR EAST DURING THE YEARS 1889-1898, INCLUSIVE.

(From the Statistics of the U. S. Treasury Department.)

COUNTRIES.	\multicolumn{10}{c}{YEAR ENDING JUNE 30.}									
	1889.	1890.	1891.	1892.	1893.	1894.	1895.	1896.	1897.	1898.
Asia.										
China:										
Imports	$17,028,412	$16,260,471	$19,321,850	$20,483,291	$20,636,535	$17,135,028	$20,515,829	$22,023,004	$20,403,862	$20,326,436
Exports	2,791,128	2,946,209	6,701,068	5,663,497	3,909,457	5,862,426	3,603,810	6,921,933	11,924,433	9,992,894
British East Indies:										
Imports	20,029,601	20,804,319	23,356,969	24,773,107	25,968,551	14,829,661	21,266,013	20,370,558	20,567,122	27,238,459
Exports	4,330,413	4,555,979	4,400,103	3,674,307	3,152,750	4,329,103	2,853,941	3,225,368	3,844,911	4,695,855
Dutch East Indies:										
Imports	5,207,254	5,791,250	6,778,992	6,914,743	8,696,588	11,276,725	7,727,282	14,854,026	15,604,866	14,529,335
Exports	2,249,604	1,799,306	2,102,942	1,372,035	1,183,605	1,722,876	1,147,315	1,576,316	2,094,109	1,201,574
French East Indies:										
Imports	319,427	93,157	14							
Exports			188,629	140,427	156,020	193,049	69,136	78,158	135,183	152,265
Portuguese East Indies:										
Imports		3,147	278					163,955		
Exports								603	519	
Hong Kong:										
Imports	1,480,266	569,745	563,275	763,323	878,078	892,511	776,476	1,419,124	923,842	746,517
Exports	3,686,384	4,439,153	4,768,697	4,894,049	4,216,602	4,209,847	4,253,040	4,691,201	6,060,039	6,265,200
Japan:										
Imports	16,687,992	21,103,324	19,309,198	23,790,202	27,454,220	19,426,522	23,695,957	25,537,038	24,009,756	25,223,610
Exports	4,619,985	5,232,643	4,807,693	3,290,111	3,195,494	3,986,815	4,634,717	7,089,685	13,255,478	20,388,420
Korea:										
Imports				608	79		100	82	509	125,936
Exports								32		
Russia, Asiatic:										
Imports	110,538	103,258	103,567	320,167	381,919	355,476	441,013	246,649	201,421	111,050
Exports	109,188	128,803	161,580	120,200	145,591	163,855	204,937	568,002	413,942	618,015

such a barrier to the development of the country. All writers and observers agree that the Chinaman as an individual is competent and industrious, possessing in some respects more sterling qualities of manhood than the Japanese, and that it is only the hopeless political degradation that keeps him reduced to the lowest industrial plane, his opportunities now being restricted to agricultural pursuits, peddling, and performing the functions of the beast of burden.

3. The introduction of Western civilization and government will stimulate mining, manufacturing, mechanical, transportation, and all the modern occupations which increase personal remuneration, add to the volume of circulation, and create demand and market for articles of civilized commerce now unknown to the people.

One may pooh-pooh at the quantity of cotton goods and bric-a-brac which constitutes the present commerce of China, but the world knows that the vast area of that decrepit empire is to be net-worked with railroads and telegraph lines opening up the vast mineral resources which are demanded in the world's arts and industries, and in these lines we shall find our opportunities for profit. European control of China means opportunity for the young men we are educating in our technical colleges, market for our iron and machinery, and untold profit for our people. Continued Chinese methods present not one ray of hope for our material profit.

No one can deny the advantage to our commerce of having Western civilization on the Eastern shore of the Pacific. It will stimulate our merchant marine, upbuild our Pacific Coast, appreciate the importance of our island stations and round out our nationality. What the Atlantic without Europe on the other side would be, the Pacific now is to us with China as it is.

"Where will the increase in our export trade be sought?" asks Mr. Ford. This question is as applicable to all the rest of the world as well as for China. Expansion of trade is a matter which concerns the individual merchant. He must seek and procure his own orders.

The argument that every ton of metal wrought in China will reduce the necessity of importing metal wares from other countries is not essentially correct. The Chinese may make plates and utensils or other crude manufactures of metal, but Americans can make machinery, and in the mechanical education of this country we have a monopoly of capital with which China will not be able to compete for a hundred years even though we made no further progress in that epoch. American mining machinery excels that of any other country and holds its own throughout the world, and the first American spade that enters the undeveloped ore banks of China will stimulate a demand for American mining machinery that will be of multiple effect in increasing our trade in that product. Not only this, but American brain and technical skill will predominate in the development of those mines and American element introduced into China will sympathetically aid trade in other directions.

The trade of the United States while measured in aggregates to be understood must be considered by particles. It is the smallest individual retail purchase that creates the demand for goods. The pending events will undoubtedly better the purchasing power of the Chinese individual, and this is a side of the question which deserves some consideration. The future extension of our trade in foreign countries, China included, must depend much more upon individual exertion than upon governmental aid. Our merchants and manufacturers must win patronage by supplying the best quality of goods at the lowest prices. Such articles will win against the most despicable governmental barriers. If we wish to sell agricultural implements to lands where they use the machete instead of the plough, we must make the best machetes possible and they will win for themselves a market. I seriously think that study of the foreign marts and needs by our manufacturers now would be much more profitable than our contemplation of the political horizon of China in which we are not apt to have a part.

Let us inquire a little further into the so-called open and closed-door policies of the European nations in the far East. These are merely the old questions of protection and free trade. Nations endeavor to expand their territory for the benefit of commerce and national development. When territory comes under the protection of the French, the Italian, the German, or any other flag than the English flag, the protective policy of the respective countries will be put in force. It is alleged that the closed door or protection policy is a subterfuge of the weak, a relic of the barbaric days of civilization. We are told that if the European nations secure

China all of them except England will monopolize it to our exclusion and slam the door of trade in our faces. There is much needless alarm in this subject. There has been much more noise than action and much more fright than fact. It is largely the old cry of wolf! uttered by a sister nation which is more interested in the question than we and whose interests are more endangered than our own. This is nothing more than the policy which we ourselves have practiced against all other nations for many years. It is true that from a higher theoretical point of view this "closed door" policy is less desirable than that of the open door. It is oftentimes an irritating and from a humanitarian point of view an extremely selfish policy. But we certainly occupy an anomalous position when we stand for the open door abroad and the closed door at home.

Instead of becoming panic-stricken by the prospect of the trade of China being placed under the protective policy of European nations, we should contemplate more calmly what the effects of such action will be. The nations engaged in this division have been enforcing this same policy against us in Europe for years. In all European countries except Great Britain the doors of trade are as tightly closed against us as they are or will be in China. Yet in some manner our trade has managed to pass their protective barriers and they collectively consume nearly one-half our products. The Germans in Europe consume $124,-000,000 worth, or fifteen times as much as the Chinese; France, $56,000,000; Belgium, $32,000,000; Netherlands, $50,000,000; Italy, $21,000,000 and Russia $8,000,000. These are all closed-door countries and yet Italy, our next smallest customer among them, with its population of 32,000,000, consumes twice as much of our products as China with its 400,000,000 people. In other words each Italian subject is worth to our trade as much as twelve Chinamen in their present condition.

We do not get a dollar's worth of trade from Europe or any other land that prejudice and intention would not prevent if it could. What is true for Europe is true for China. China will never take from us that which we cannot supply better and cheaper than other nations. In her present deplorable state she will never take much more from us than she now takes and our only hope of increased trade with her lies in the betterment of her civilization.

What the future political relations of the United States will be in the affairs of the far East no one can prophesy. Protection of trade and subjects is the duty of the nation. Our commercial interests do not necessarily involve or necessitate political complications such as the expansion of our territory beyond what has already been acquired as a result of the war with Spain. Public opinion in this country does not desire that the United States should acquire one foot of Chinese territory. Of necessity our policy must be one of drift and observation.

For the present we can only jealously guard such rights as we have acquired and be prepared to avail ourselves of all future opportunities, endeavoring through diplomacy to maintain such friendly political relations as will secure equal rights for our goods in competition with those of other nations and the protection of the interests of our citizens who seek investment there.

This country within the past few years has made some notable commercial conquests without the acquirement of territory or the suggestion thereof. We have commercially invaded Mexico and become supreme in that field of trade, forcing our goods into her markets which were previously hostile and securing business opportunities of incalculable value. In South Africa, a country which a few years ago seemed more hopeless as a field of trade than the far East, we have found a grand market for our food stuffs and our machinery.

The interests of the United States in the far East will be protected and benefited by the friendly relations which we hold with the two greatest countries now engaged in partitioning China. Both Russia and England hold us to most cordial relations and neither country would dare to discriminate against us in any unusual or unjust way. Both desire to retain our friendship and under these amicable conditions there is great diplomatic opportunity for us.

Every foot of the outer world thus far acquired by England has been to our benefit. Although our chief competitor in the manufacture of textiles, ship-building, etc., this country is nearest to us in blood and ideals and to-day England is one of our chief customers, taking nearly fifty per cent of all that we send abroad. She takes over half of our European exports. Our British neighbors on the north consume twice as much of our products as the rest of North America and more of South America combined. British

Oceanica takes nearly as much from us as China and Japan combined, while we send to the British in Africa three times as much as we do to all the other people of the dark continent. It is but natural that our sympathies should lead us to desire that as much of China as possible should fall under English rule.

DISCUSSION.

JOHN FOORD, ESQ., *New York City, Secretary, American Asiatic Association.*

I have been profoundly impressed with the ability and industry displayed in the preparation of the papers to which we have just listened, and I must pay a special tribute of respect to the earnest intention of their authors to set before you, fairly and impartially, the conditions affecting our commercial relations with the far East. But the fact can hardly have escaped you that the main lines of argument which these papers follow are mutually destructive, and to that extent have relieved me of saying a good deal in reply that might, otherwise, have been necessary. Mr. Ford takes a discouraging view of the future of our trade with China, because he regards the dismemberment of that empire as inevitable, and Mr. Hill takes an optimistic view of it for precisely the same reason. I am in entire agreement with Mr. Ford that our Chinese trade would be a diminishing instead of an increasing quantity if China is to be partitioned into spheres of commercial influence, in most of which we should encounter a hostile tariff, and in all of which there would be a pressure, silently but constantly exercised, in favor of other merchandise than our own. I disagree absolutely with Mr. Hill, and therein I think I voice the sentiments of all Americans who have trade relations with the far East, in assuming that no matter what may be the commercial policy of the powers to whom the control of the Celestial Empire will pass, we should succeed not only in holding our own there, but in greatly increasing our present average of business, simply because of the transformation that the dominance of any form of European civilization would effect in that mass of humanity which we call China. The experience of Madagascar is too recent in the business of our manufacturers and exporters of cotton textiles, to admit of any illusions on that point. Here was a trade in which a most promising beginning had been made in 1897, with exports, chiefly in drills and sheetings, of some $550,000, but which one year of French sovereignty, with its accompanying tariff and other methods of exclusion has completely wiped out. I don't think we should have any better chance with the French "sphere" in China, than we have now in Madagascar; I doubt if we should fare much better in the German "sphere," and if we held on to our cotton trade in North China, in spite of the application of a Russian tariff, it would only be till the protected and bounty-fed Moscow manufacturer was able to produce for eleven cents what we are ready to sell for seven cents. A differential of 60 per cent is quite too high a burden on trade to give the producer against whom it operated much of an opportunity.

But I take issue both with Mr. Ford and Mr. Hill in assuming the dismemberment of China to be inevitable. That seems to me to be taking something for granted which we cannot possibly allow to be taken for granted, in short, it seems like begging the whole question at issue. The partition of China among the great powers of the earth, and the consequent girdling of the Chinese coast with a rampart of foreign custom houses, involves certain questions which the people of the United States have not yet passed upon, and which will be answered pretty much as these people may choose to direct. In other words, if the people of this republic make up their minds that the partition of China would be contrary to their interests, the partition of China will not take place.

Let us clearly understand the situation as it exists to-day: There are two great powers, Russia and France, whose interests impel them to work for the division of China into zones of exclusive commercial influence, if not into zones of actual political and military control. Neither of these nations produces anything which China needs, in great quantity at least, which cannot be more cheaply produced by its rivals. An open market in China, therefore, means for them next to no market at all, and their influence is necessarily thrown on the side of fencing off markets by the aid of a protective wall of customs duties. There is a third great power whose citizens have shown their ability to hold their own in the commercial competition of the world, but whose attitude in China may best be described as that of waiting to see how the cat is going to jump. On what must be called a frivolous pretext, Germany obtained a footing in Shantung, in the shape of a lease of the land around the entrance of Kiaochau Bay—an acquisition which Herr Von Brandt has euphemistically described as a place in the sunshine by the side of others who are basking in it. The same authority—a former German Minister to China—says: "Far from wishing to restrict the area within which foreign trade and industry can and ought to flourish in China, she (Germany) will ever advocate the maintenance and extension of commercial relations with the Chinese Empire—not to the exclusion of others, but for the general benefit of humanity. And there is no reason why she should not co-operate to that end with any power animated by the same wishes and aspirations." It must be admitted, however, that Germany stands for equality of commercial opportunity in China with a difference, since she has cautiously reserved for her own manufacturers and capitalists the exclusive right to construct railroads, work mines, and, generally speaking, develop the resources of a province half the size of Prussia and a third more populous. Per contra, Kiaochau has been declared a free port.

If there be any doubt as to which side the interests of Germany impel her to take in the struggle to keep the door open to commerce in China, there can be none as to the position which traditional policy and present needs alike require England to occupy. It is quite probable that there are Englishmen of light and leading, both in the political and commercial world, who regard, like my friend, Mr. Ford, the partition of China as inevitable and who are, therefore, resigned to the necessity of at once marking out the English sphere of influence and making preparations to defend it against all comers. But it remains as true to-day, as it was a year ago, when the Duke of Devonshire made the declaration in the House of Lords, "that the principle, and the sole principle, which Her Majesty's Government have had in view in their dealings with China—the principle which has actuated both their declarations at home and their communications with foreign powers—has been that China should remain open to commerce as now, that the facilities at present possessed by British subjects for trading in China and for the employment of British capital in China should not be diminished, but should rather be increased, and that no facilities, no concessions in these directions, which may be made to other powers, should be denied to British subjects." It may be, as Mr. Ford says, that not one of the foreign nations who occupy positions around the coast of China has any interest in maintaining the integrity of the empire "unless such maintenance can prevent rivals from securing more than a fair share of the spoils." But there is much significance in that "unless," and it would seem to be hardly necessary to assume that the desire to secure a fair share of the trade of China must fall under the same ban as a desire to secure this trade plus a slice of territory. The spoil of military aggression is not precisely the same thing as the fruits of open commercial competition, even if the freedom of that competition has to be assured by a display of superior force.

And here, let me say, that Mr. Hill does not seem correctly to apprehend how much freedom commerce enjoys in China to-day. There is no "Chinese Wall," in his sense of the phrase, and one by one the obstacles which have been interposed to trade in the interior of the empire are disappearing. Viewed from one side, there are many and irritating obstructions to anything like free commercial exchange between the foreign merchant and the people of China, but, considering how hard and fast must be the hold of tradition over an empire that has long outlived all the ancient civilizations of the world, perhaps the wonder should be, not that the process of change is slow and difficult in China, but that it has gone on of late years with such rapidity. The Chinese tariff is a uniform *ad valorem* duty of 5 per cent, payable in silver, and that is a very trifling burden on commerce compared with the tariff which Russia, France or Germany would impose, when the time came to convert a sphere of influence into a sphere of sovereignty. So far as our treaty rights are concerned, we stand on precisely the same footing as these powers do in China to-day—we enjoy the equality of commercial opportunity known as the "open door," and under such conditions we have no misgivings about the future of our trade. But if there is to be dismemberment, we can have neither part nor lot in it; we have everything to lose and nothing to gain by the division of the empire. We might profit by the liberal policy of Great Britain within what would naturally be her sphere, though that is not where we have had most trade up to the present time; but elsewhere our trade would be at the mercy of whatever discriminating tariff might be declared against it.

"Is it consistent," asks Mr. Hill, "to stand for the open door abroad while maintaining a closed door at home?" It is a habit of English-speaking people not to trouble themselves much about the logical sequence of any line of public policy. For reasons sufficient to themselves, the people of the United States have adopted a protective tariff for the better development of their domestic industries. When they find sufficient reason to dispense with this tariff, it will go like the scaffolding of a completed building, which has served its purpose. There are some of us who think that most of the protective features of the tariff might be dispensed with now, but I take it that our individual views on that subject have nothing to do with the demand that everybody should occupy the same commercial footing in China. That is a matter also which vitally concerns our interests, and while we can have nothing to say about the efforts of Russia, France and Germany to imitate our protective policy at home, we have the clearest possible right to lodge a protest against the application of their domestic tariff to a country in which they have no more rights than are possessed by ourselves.

I must, therefore, doubly take exception to Mr. Ford's phrase about the United States being pitched unexpectedly into this "circle of marauding powers." I am not concerned with the defence of British policy in China, except in so far as it appears to be the only policy that the United States can support, and it may thus be proper to discriminate between a power that takes a naval station in Chinese waters as a base for the dismemberment of the empire, and one that takes a station opposite it for the purpose of preventing that dismemberment. Then, as to the unexpectedness of our position in China; is it not a fact that we were face to face with precisely the same problems which present themselves to-day, before there was any thought of taking Manila and possessing ourselves of the Philippines? I admit that had we no interests in China, the possession of the Philippines would be meaningless, but the Chinese question came before the Philippine, not after it, either in time or logical sequence. In December, 1897, it became evident that a situation had been created under which the trade and treaty rights secured by the United States in China might be seriously imperilled. These had already been adversely affected by the agreement made in regard to the Russo-Manchurian Railway, in which it was provided that "goods imported from Russia into China by rail and exported from China to Russia in the same manner shall pay respectively an import or export Chinese duty to the extent of one-third less as compared with the duty imposed at Chinese seaport custom houses." That must be held to be in clear contravention of the provision of the treaty of 1844 which reads: "Citizens of the United States resorting to China for the purpose of commerce will pay the duties of import and export prescribed in the tariff which is fixed by and made part of this treaty. They shall in no case be subject to other or higher duties than are or shall be required of the people of any other nation whatever, and if additional advantages and privileges of whatever description be conceded hereafter by China to any other nation the United States and the citizens thereof shall be entitled thereupon to a complete, equal and impartial participation in the same."

The existing status had been further threatened by the virtual supremacy of Russia in Manchuria and the Liaotung peninsula and the consequent danger that the treaty port of Newchwang—more than half of whose imports of cotton textiles come from the United States—might at any time be declared a part of the Russian Empire, and therefore subject to its tariff. In short, the beginnings were only too obvious of a process of alienation of sovereignty under which the whole of North China might pass under the dominion of the Czar. As it happens that 80 per cent of all the cotton drills, and over 90 per cent of all the sheetings which the United States exports to China, find their way to the three northern treaty ports of Tientsin, Chefoo and Newchwang, this was a process to which the manufacturing interests of our country could hardly be indifferent. The first body to take action in regard to the threatening situation in China was the New York Chamber of Commerce, to which a very largely signed petition had been addressed, calling upon the chamber "to take such immediate action in the premises as may be deemed expedient and proper, to the end that the present situation may be brought to the attention of the Department of State at Washington, and that the important interests of the United States, together with existing treaty rights of its citizens in China, may be duly and promptly further safeguarded." At its meeting in February, 1898, the New York Chamber of Commerce addressed a memorial to the President of the United States in which it was set forth that the trade of the United States with China is rapidly increasing, and is destined with the further opening of that country to assume large proportions, unless arbitrarily debarred by the action of foreign governments. In view of the changes threatening the future development of this trade, the chamber respectfully and earnestly urged that such proper steps be taken as might commend themselves to the wisdom of the President, "for the prompt and energetic defence of the existing treaty rights of our citizens in China, and for the preservation and protection of their important commercial interests in that empire." Similar action was taken by the Chambers of Commerce of Philadelphia, Boston and San Francisco, and the whole subject of American interests in the far East was fairly lifted into the place of commercial and public importance which it is so fully entitled to occupy.

That fateful first of May, when Dewey's guns destroyed constructions more antique than Spanish men-of-war, did undoubtedly give to the people of the United States a new sense of their nearness to the scene of the strife of international ambitions in the far East, and probably brought home to them a new perception of the impossibility of remaining indifferent to the issue of that struggle. But it did not make manifest, for the first time, the fact that no question of our generation is of such vital moment for the present and future welfare of the American people as this of the preservation of equality of opportunity in a market comprising one-fourth of the entire human race. "We must have a market or we shall have revolution," is Senator Frye's blunt way of stating that the productive capacity of the country has so far outrun its capacity to consume that a foreign outlet for our surplus products is an absolute necessity to the peaceful growth of the republic. This brings us to a consideration of what is, perhaps, the main question: What is the value of China as a market? The experience of the past affords but a slender test of that value. And yet there has been, of late years, a very considerable expansion of our export trade with China. Between 1887 and 1897 there was an increase of 121 per cent in the quantity and of 59½ in the value of our cotton fabrics which that market absorbed. In the same period the imports of American kerosene oil into China increased from 13,613,090 gallons to 48,212,505 gallons. In 1887 the imports of plain gray and white cotton piece goods from the United States into China represented 14½ per cent in quantity and 22½ per cent in value of the whole importation of the year; in 1897 the proportion had advanced to 29½ per cent in quantity and 33 per cent in value. That this trade is a steadily increasing one is shown by the reports of the Bureau of Statistics for the first eight months of the current fiscal year, from which it appears that while the export to China for the corresponding period of 1897 was 85,351,867 yards of cotton cloth valued at $4,828,852, it was, from the first of July to the twenty-eighth of February last, 135,604,310 yards, valued at $6,080,355—an increase in two years of 59 per cent in quantity and 27 per cent in value. These figures ought to be a sufficient answer to Mr. Ford's question: "How can cotton goods of the United States make other than a limited market in Asia against the cottons of India, Japan and China?" As a matter of fact, in cotton drills and sheetings the market of North China is already ours, to have and to hold, without any effective competition whatever.

But it is the testimony of every one who has studied the question on the spot that only the surface of this market has been scratched. Mr. Ford quotes a statement of the members of the Blackburn Mission as to the poverty of the Chinese, but he does not quote their general conclusion : "China's trade possibilities are immeasurable. The sparing use and non-presence of foreign commodities are warrant enough of future expansion, if a policy could be adopted which shall open up the entire country to the advantages of unrestricted commercial intercourse." Mr. Ford says that instead of wanting cottons, China will utilize her own resources, but forgets the shrewd comment of the men from Blackburn : "The establishment of permanent industries need not cause us too much alarm. They must be understood as meaning a source of regular income by which the purchasing power of the people is increased, and as powerful factors in that developement by which in the long run we shall most assuredly profit." Mr. Ford quotes Colquhoun to show that the commerce of Hong Kong with Europe exhibits a tendency to decrease, but fails to quote his judgment on the whole commercial situation in China : "What the utilization of China would mean can only be realized by a full appreciation of the extraordinary resources of that country judged from various points of view. She has the men to create armies and navies; the materials, especially iron and coal, requisite for the purpose of railways and steam navigation; all the elements in fact to build up a great living force. One thing alone is wanting—the will, the directing power—which, absent from within, is now being applied from without . . . . . And when it is understood that not merely the soil, rich and fertile, but that the mineral resources—the greatest, perhaps, in the world—are as yet practically untouched, the merest surface being scratched; when we consider the extent of China's population; the ability and enterprise, and, above all, the intense vitality of the people, as strong as ever after four millenniums; when we reflect on the general characteristics of the race, is it not clear that the Chinese, under direction, are destined to dominate the whole of Eastern Asia, and maybe to play a leading part in the affairs of the world?"

To that estimate scores might be added to prove the fallacy of Mr. Ford's idea that China is a "decayed and decaying empire." The phrase might be justly applied to the ruling class of China, though the recent reform movement so abruptly repressed by the Empress Dowager shows that the elements of change are working even in high places. Nor does Mr. Ford correctly apprehend the possibilities of the Chinaman when he speaks of him as hopelessly bigoted and a hater of all progress. All who have studied his character agree with Colquhoun that, though clannish and conservative, the Chinaman is remarkably free from prejudice, religious or political, especially in matters of tangible interest. He has no objection to purchasing the article which he judges to be cheapest and best, wherever it may come from; or, as Bourne remarks, "the Chinaman has everywhere a taste for luxury; he may be trusted to buy luxuries to the full extent of his means. It is this quality which will some day make the foreign trade of China of gigantic dimensions."

Here, then, is great empire, awakening from the slumber of centuries, and over which the age of steam and electricity has, so far, passed without transforming it, waiting to be equipped with all that constitutes the appliances of modern civilization. It possesses the greatest coal deposits in the world, and yet its transport facilities are so crude that anthracite, which costs thirty-three cents per ton among the hills at the mine at Pingting-chau, costs $17 at the entrance to the plain, after being carried eighty miles on the back of asses—an addition of twenty cents per ton per mile to the original cost. Labor is cheap among these Chinese millions, but the product of labor is dear, because the effectiveness of the man plus the machine has not been developed. Nowhere else in the world is there such a reservoir of untouched wealth as in China, side by side with an industrious and docile population ready, under proper direction, to utilize it. The great nations of the world are pressing forward to get their share of the rich returns which will attend the opening up of the resources of China. Here, as elsewhere, there is no longer any international politics, in the old sense of the term; the diplomatic questions of the hour relate, simply and solely, to international trade. Mr. Ford asks: "How can American iron and steel enter markets held to be closed by

European countries, each one of which wishes to keep for its own people the construction of the railroads, the building and running of steam vessels and the profits of the custom house?" But suppose that the United States serves a notice on the European countries which would like to divide China between them that it has treaty rights there, any infringement of which would be regarded as much a hostile act as if it were an attack upon its territory? Do you suppose that with this new and formidable accession to the support of the policy of the open door in China there would be any likelihood of the policy of commercial exclusion being pushed to the limit?

It is, therefore, somewhat beside the question to inquire what is to happen when each port is under a different head, and competing with one another after the fashion peculiar to five rival governments, because the very essence of the contention is that it rests with the Government of the United States to prevent precisely that eventuality. There are lions in the path, no doubt; there always are in the way of national progress. But if we are to turn aside from the path, plainly marked out for us in the natural line of commercial advance, because of certain traditions of foreign policy, which we are asked to regard as no less sacred than the Constitution of the United States, then we must, perforce, make up our minds to be content with the sphere of national growth for which the purely continental policy was avowedly adopted. At a time when Shanghai is nearer San Francisco than New Orleans used to be to New York, it would seem to be necessary to expand the diplomacy of our grandfathers and frankly to recognize that it is quite as essential to the well-being of the United States of to-day that China should remain an open market, as it was seventy years ago that the colonial system of Europe should not take a new hold on the Republics of Central and South America.

There is nothing insoluble in what is called the problem of internal taxation in China which so many people find to be an insuperable obstacle to the expansion of international trade. The one valid asset which the Chinese Empire offers to-day to the foreign lender is the income of the imperial maritime customs, administered for these many years by an Englishman, Sir Robert Hart, and administered without the slightest taint of "squeeze" or discrimination. The internal transit tax—the likin—has been and is a fruitful source of corruption, but in several provinces its collection has already been transferred to the control of the maritime customs, and the same methods will be applied as hitherto governed the collection of tariff duties. It may be safely asserted that the results will justify, and probably facilitate, the further extension of foreign control over the most important part of the internal tax system of the empire.

If we are to deal with China as the ward of civilization, and not as a carcass over which the vultures of military aggression may struggle, a good many difficulties that now appear insuperable will disappear before the united and vigorous action of the Powers enlisted in the cause of peaceful progress. The main question is, shall the United States be a party to this work of progressive civilization in China, or shall it respond to the call for aid with a helpless *non possumus*, because the fathers were wise enough to construct a formula admirably suited to their time, which their sons are not courageous enough to adapt to the larger demands of a different age?

Dr. W. P. Wilson, *Director of the Commercial Museum, Philadelphia.*

I am going to confine my remarks to just two points, and will be brief, as I can say, with Mr. Foord, that most of the arguments have been presented on both.

The first point is this: I am going to quote a sentence from Mr. Hill's paper which I believe to be the keynote of the securing of all foreign trade: "Expansion of export trade depends upon individual exertion."

Just to give you one or two points on that. We know very well the extensive and aggressive line of cotton manufacture that has taken place in England, and, as our manufacturing interests have grown up, it would not naturally be supposed that we would have a great cotton export trade, especially in England or the Continent, so closely situated to the greatest cotton manufacturing country in the world.

In Philadelphia there exists a progressive cotton manufacturing plant, which in one particular line has secured an extremely large trade in both London and Paris.

There has been a great deal said, in the papers at least, and in discussions that have taken place recently in New York and elsewhere, toward stirring up this question of the Oriental trade, with reference to Japan and China, and the danger, as these two countries become more civilized and more active in manufactures, of fulfilling their own needs in their own manufactures. I want to give you just one point with reference to that; I want to say that I feel there is not the slightest danger of that and that the trade we shall secure in the Orient depends upon individual effort.

In 1889 we exported to England nearly thirty-two million dollars' ($32,000,000) worth of manufactured goods. In 1898 we exported to England seventy-four millions ($74,000,000) of manufactured goods. Now in all this time England had become more and more active in her own lines of manufacture, and we, as a growing manufacturing nation had more than doubled our export of manufactured goods into England.

The same with Germany. She has come to an immense period of activity in manufacturing, overtopping England in many markets of the world; taking away from England, in many lines of manufacture, her prestige; and within the last year and a half being the cause of a meeting called by Mr. Chamberlain to examine into the whole question of why British trade was declining, and why Germany, the United States and other countries were taking her place to a certain extent.

To Germany in 1878 we exported sixteen and one-half million ($16,500,000) dollars' worth of manufactured goods and products. In 1898 we had doubled that. We sent over to her thirty-two millions seven hundred thousand dollars' ($32,700,000) worth of manufactured goods right in the face of her activity. I say that was due almost absolutely to individual effort and individual study of the market of Germany, and the needs there. They manufacture what they need. We manufacture it a little better, a little finer, put little touches here and there which take the market. And that is what we shall have to do all over the world.

It has been the same with France. In 1889 we sent over a little over five million dollars' worth of manufactured goods and in 1898 nearly twenty-four millions right in the face of her activities. One item we sent into Paris was Turkish towels, manufactured in Philadelphia. Why? Because we manufactured a finer grade than they manufacture in any of the mills of England.

To Belgium in 1889 we sent nearly three millions' worth. In 1898 we sent over nine millions (9,000,000). See the progress.

I simply bring out these points to show that the markets of the Orient are ours if we will study them, and if individual effort is made to capture them. They are not ours unless we go to them. I had prepared a little more in that line, but I am going to let that go.

One word on the Philippines, and the work of those islands. In the first place I believe these new territorial provinces, that, I do not want to say we are acquiring, but which are under our care at the present time, are doing a great deal of missionary work for us.

We are all perfectly well aware of the fact that we are not, as formerly, carrying our own goods abroad. I think we all feel a little ashamed of that. Forty years ago 90 per cent of our manufactures were going abroad in our own bottoms. At the present moment only 20 per cent is carried by our own ships. I wonder if any one has stopped to think of the cause of this, or of the revenue paid to England and Germany for carrying our goods.

Last year three hundred million dollars were paid to foreign shipping interests to carry our exports to Europe and elsewhere. That is nine millions more than the manufactures which we sent over to Europe amounted to.

We sent abroad, all told, last year twelve hundred and forty-eight million dollars' worth of manufactured and raw products, and out of that we sent over to Europe, about, I believe, two hundred and ninety-one millions, but the cost of our shipping from this country, which was outside of our own shipping, was over three hundred millions.

Now the point I want to make there is this: We have broadened out wonderfully since we have possessed a little interest in Porto Rico, Cuba and the Philippines. We are actually sending our own transports and ships to the Philippines, and carrying the mail, and are about carrying our goods to the near West India Islands. It is to be hoped that we will develop a habit of doing that, of studying the necessities of the trade with different parts of the world, and of building our own ships and doing our own shipping. It is to be hoped we shall remove the obstructive laws that have taken all our shipping off the seas. I think the acquiring of the Philippine Islands and other provinces will be a missionary work in the study of the question.

Again, did you ever think of the cost to us—what we pay for not having foreign banks in the countries where we do business? London is the centre of a banking system which has branches in every quarter of the globe, and Great Britain pays tribute to nobody. We pay tribute in doing business with England of about one-half of 1 per cent, and we paid out a great many million dollars last year for the privilege of doing our banking business through London. I am in hopes that this acquisition of territory will be a missionary effort in this direction. We will have our own banks in Porto Rico, Cuba and possibly in the Philippines, and this experience may give us a leaning in that direction, for as soon as we begin to study the question practically we will see how much money we are losing.

I believe the Philippine Islands will be of great advantage to us as a distributing centre for the Eastern trade. With the eight or nine hundred millions of inhabitants that border around the Orient, and the seven hundred and seventy-five millions of export material that goes in there, we furnish only forty millions. It looks as if we were now about to have our opportunity, and if we put individual interest into it, there is no reason why we should not, at least take our share of it from Great Britain, Germany and Belgium, and have three or four hundred millions instead of forty.

I believe that the Philippine Islands will take us over and lead us to do that.

The Philippine Islands themselves I believe to be immensely valuable. There is no richer spot on the face of the globe, covering, as it does, an area equal to New England, New York and Pennsylvania. It is wholly tropical; everything can be cultivated there that can be cultivated in any tropical country. The main products of the islands can be increased a hundredfold with the use of the arts and appliances of civilization. It would be amusing if I should give you some of the methods in which sugar is raised and manufactured in the Philippines, and I doubt whether, if the sugar was not entirely changed in the process of refining, you would want to eat any of it.

COMMERCIAL RELATIONS WITH THE FAR EAST. 157

Fifteen or twenty years ago the Philippine Islands raised a great many million dollars' worth of coffee. To-day, or last year, only twenty-four thousand dollars' worth of coffee got outside of the Philippines. That is one of the most promising crops that might be raised in those islands. It would be just as valuable as the coffee of Java had the islands been peopled with an intelligent people capable of coping with the disasters which in every country come to crops. The coffee crop of the Philippines was entirely ruined by an insect, and it has been practically given up. The only crop encouraged by the Spaniards was tobacco, out of which they made a great revenue. Cotton-growing would also be extremely profitable. Manila hemp is perhaps the leading crop at the present moment from which we receive four or five million dollars a year, and which, if properly cultivated and properly studied, and the quality improved, could be made tenfold more valuable than now.

I want to state that I believe that the foothold we have obtained in the Orient will lead us to study the whole question. We will introduce civilized methods into those islands which will bring out the value—put our own sugar machinery in for that which is one hundred and fifty years old, antiquated and useless, introduce our own economic plans and ideas, and in that way increase the output and quality, and in time make one of the most valuable spots on the face of the globe of the Philippine Islands. At the same time being in the Orient, studying the whole question of foreign trade there, which is an individual study, based on individual effort, we will be able to take from other nations, not so active, perhaps, part of their trade, and as China and Japan grow in civilization, and need ten, or a hundred or a thousand fold of the civilized products they now need, we shall be on the ground ready and able to supply those needs.

Professor E. R. JOHNSON, *University of Pennsylvania.*

The purpose of this session of the American Academy is to discuss our commercial prospects in the East and the factors affecting them. The Hawaiian and Philippine Islands are factors that will influence our Pacific trade, but they are only two of many forces and a consideration of their influence is incidental rather than fundamental to the discussion in hand. These two groups of newly-acquired island possessions are attracting so much attention at the present time that we are in danger of making the double mistake of overestimating the commercial importance of the islands and of neglecting to study other and possibly more important factors that are to affect our Pacific trade.

In criticism of Mr. Ford's paper I would say that I sympathize with the general spirit and method of his study. There are so many loose and exaggerated statements current regarding the prospective expansion of our Pacific trade and the quickening influences that our new possessions are to exert that we need to have our assertions subjected to critical analysis, and Mr. Ford is a master of that art. However the man who loves analysis strongly may neglect synthesis; and I think Mr. Ford's study does not construct so many castles of hope as the facts warrant us in building. I shall endeavor to illustrate this by criticising one point in the paper.

From his survey of the industrial and commercial conditions, present and probable, of China, Mr. Ford concludes that China will increase her exports largely, but that she will not have occasion to import much, and of what she does import we shall have but a small share. As he says "Of the imports into China, cotton goods hold the first place, opium the second, rice the third and metal manufactures and mineral oils are of equal importance, as fourth and fifth on the list. In no one item of this enumeration has the United States a natural monopoly; and in only one (petroleum) has it a partial monopoly, fast being impaired; and in two (rice and petroleum) it has and can have no share." These statements are true, and they seem to predict a sorry place for us in Chinese markets, but possibly they do not present the whole of the case. I think there is probably a stronger prospect than this picture indicates that American manufacturers will be able for some time to come to sell cottons and metal wares in China in competition with rival producers; of that however I will not speak; but will consider the probability of our being able to find larger markets for our food products in China. Is there reason to expect that Japan, China and Eastern Asia will furnish a considerable market for American cereals?

The answer to this question must depend in part upon whether China is or is not going to pass through an industrial revolution. I agree with Mr. Ford that there is every indication that "China will not remain as she is. France, Germany, Italy, England, Russia—these nations have gone to Asia for a purpose. They intend to build railroads, open and develop mines, establish industries, and secure all they can from a careful attention to encouraging competition on Asiatic conditions."

Mr. Ford also expects that China will manufacture largely and import but small quantities. He says: "In place of wanting cottons, products of iron and steel, or other metals, or rice, China will utilize her own resources. This may be a work of time, but under the stimulus of so many competitors it will not require many years to bring it to pass. Every ton of iron, of copper or of tin wrought into metal ware in China; every pound of wool or of cotton, or of silk made into cloth in the provinces, will reduce the necessity of importing them from other countries."

As regards one thing all observers of what is going on in the East are agreed; China is going to be controlled by occidental nations, and her natural resources of great value and variety are to be exploited. Concerning the development of textile manufacturing industries in China the future is not quite so certain; but the present indications are, as Mr. Ford suggests, that there are to be many cotton mills established in China. If the coal and iron and other mineral resources of China are exploited—of course it will be by native labor—and if a considerable portion of the population becomes engaged in manufacturing, certain results are certain to follow; population will increase in numbers, the percentage of the population devoted to the production of foods will decrease, and the necessity for importing food will increase. China is now a large importer of food—rice being third in the list of imports; in the future she will be obliged to import more largely. China is now such a thickly settled country that these industrial changes must place her in the list of nations that depend upon foreign countries for a considerable portion of their food supply.

Is this imported food going to consist exclusively or mainly of rice? If so, then we shall not share in China's food imports very largely, at least in the proximate future. So far as I know the Oriental has no antipathy to wheat and other cereals of the temperate zone. He eats rice because it is his natural domestic crop. During the past five years our sales of wheat flour have doubled in Hong Kong, have more than doubled on the continent of Asia and have nearly quadrupled in

Japan. May not these facts be accepted as a portent of much larger sales in the future when the economic progress of the Orient is once well under way? The economic and social changes of the people of the East will be accompanied by modifications and greater variety in their wants and their general standards of living. Furthermore, the fact that the industrial and social changes are to come about under European and occidental leadership will tend to enlarge the demand for the food products of the temperate zone.

I think Mr. Ford underestimates the dynamic qualities of the individual Chinaman. He says, in contrasting the Chinese and Japanese: "A mere comparison of commercial details develops the distinction between Japan and China—a living and pushing people, and a decayed and dying empire." And he also says in another connection: "The character of the two peoples is different, and the Japanese have much higher organizing powers."

The Chinaman and the Chinese Empire have very different characteristics. The political institutions of the country are crumbling from the dry rot of ultra-conservatism and official corruption. The government seems practically incapable of change for the better; but not so the individual Chinaman. He travels freely, he is a willing and industrious artisan, and possesses to a considerable degree the power to avail himself of economic opportunities. It is true that the Japanese possess higher organizing powers; but in the economic and social changes to transpire in China the Occident is to supply the organizing needs of the Chinese. There are, in my opinion, good reasons for expecting the Chinaman to vary his wants and become an important importer. I have attempted to show one of the ways in which we are likely to participate in supplying his wants.

The Political Relations of the United States with the Far East.

Addresses.

INTRODUCTORY ADDRESS.

A REVIEW OF OUR FOREIGN POLICY IN THE FAR EAST.

By the Honorable JOHN BASSETT MOORE, *Columbia University.*

From the foundation of our government the energy and enterprise that distinguish the American character have impelled our merchants, in spite of unrivaled opportunities at home, to seek in the markets of the world an extension of their commerce. "Before the war of independence," said Mr. Jefferson, in a report made by him as secretary of state, "about one-sixth of the wheat and flour exported from the United States, and about one-fourth in value of their dried and pickled fish, and some rice, found their best markets in the Mediterranean;" and among the earliest negotiations undertaken after our independence was established were those for commercial treaties with the countries bordering on that sea. When, in 1821, the Emperor of Russia issued a ukase by which it was proposed to inhibit the right of navigation and of fishing along a vast extent of coast bordering on the Pacific Ocean, John Quincy Adams, as secretary of state, replied: "The United States can admit no part of these claims. Their right of navigation and of fishing is perfect, and has been in constant exercise from the earliest times, after the peace of 1783." And when, in 1823, the Monroe Doctrine was announced, one of its declared objects was to prevent the extension in any part of the American continents of the colonial system under which foreign commerce was restricted and excluded. Such was the policy of the United States. It sought in the commerce of the world an equality of opportunity. Its object, as tersely expressed in the recent negotiations at Paris with reference to the Philippines, was "to maintain an open door to the world's commerce."

But while our commerce with Europe and Africa, and along the shores of America, north and south, was fostered and protected, our intercourse with the East was not neglected. In the early part of this century, after the revolt of the Spanish colonies in America against the rule of Spain, a trade was carried on by American merchants between those countries and Asia, in addition to that which was conducted directly between the United States and the East. With its growth, our trade with Oriental countries attracted more and more the attention and solicitude of our government. In 1832 Edmund Roberts, a sea captain of Portsmouth, N. H., was chosen by President Jackson as an "agent for the purpose of examining in the Indian Ocean the means of extending the commerce of the United States by commercial arrangements with the powers whose dominions border on those seas;" and he was empowered to negotiate for the extension of the commerce of the United States in the Pacific. In March, 1833, he concluded a treaty of amity and commerce with Siam.

Roberts was followed by other agents of our government, who were sent on similar missions. Expeditions were dispatched for purposes of exploration and negotiation. A determined effort was made to break down the seclusion of the East, and a show of force was not deemed an inappropriate mode of disclosing the design.

An important step forward was taken when, on March 3, 1843, an act was approved by which Congress placed forty thousand dollars "at the disposal of the President . . . to enable him to establish the future commercial relations between the United States and the Chinese Empire on terms of national equal reciprocity." In the following May Caleb Cushing, one of the ablest and most accomplished diplomatists whom our country has produced, was appointed envoy extraordinary, minister plenipotentiary and commissioner to China, for the purpose of carrying this act into effect. On July 3, 1844, he concluded with that empire a general convention of peace, amity and commerce, by which the intercourse between the two countries was regulated and placed on a certain foundation.

By this treaty it was stipulated that citizens of the United States, resorting to China for the purposes of commerce, should pay the duties of import and export prescribed in a tariff thereto annexed, and that they should in no case be subject to other or higher duties than should be required of the people of any other nation. Five ports were opened, not only to the trade, but also to the residence of American citizens. Provision was made for the appointment of consuls.

In 1858 other treaties were concluded, the negotiator on the part of the United States being William B. Reed, a citizen of Philadelphia.

In June, 1861, Anson Burlingame, whose name is also memorably associated with the history of our relations with China, was sent as envoy extraordinary and minister plenipotentiary to that country. The ancient empire was then passing through a period of civil commotions which seemed to threaten its permanence. In these critical times Burlingame played a prominent and benevolent part. In a dispatch written to Mr. Seward in June, 1863, he said: "In my dispatch No. 18, of June 2, 1862, I had the honor to write, if the treaty powers could agree among themselves on the neutrality of China, and together secure order in the treaty ports, and give their moral support to that party in China in favor of order, the interests of humanity would be subserved. Upon my arrival at Peking I at once elaborated my views, and found, upon comparing them with those held by the representatives of England and Russia, that they were in accord with theirs." In June, 1864, Burlingame, acting in the spirit of his dispatch to Mr. Seward, gave instructions to the consul-general of the United States at

Shanghai as to the "extent of the rights and duties of American citizens under the treaty." These instructions he submitted to the British, French and Russian ministers, who authorized him to state that they met with their approval, both as to general views and as to policy. The policy of the instructions, as expressed by Burlingame himself, was "an effort to substitute fair diplomatic action in China for force." Of this policy Mr. Seward declared: "It is approved with much commendation."

In 1868 Burlingame, who had then resigned from the service of the United States, came to this country, in association with two Chinese officials of high rank, as the representative of the government to which he had lately been accredited. Though it is not usual for governments to receive as diplomatic agents their own citizens, he was cordially welcomed; and on July 28, 1868, he concluded the well-known treaty which has always borne his name.

Since the days of Burlingame, new questions between the two countries have from time to time arisen, as the result of conditions the full development and varying aspects of which could not be foreseen. But, in respect of China, as well as of other countries in the East, it may be said that the Government of the United States has adhered to the policy of endeavoring by "fair diplomatic action" to adjust all differences in conformity with international rights and interests.

But, in the consideration of the situation in the East, it is impossible to concentrate our vision exclusively upon the relations of the United States with the particular governments with which we have contracted treaties in that quarter of the globe. There has existed in respect of the Orient a concert of powers in which, as has been intimated, we have borne an important part, when its object was to maintain the independence and "neutrality" of governments, and by that means to assure equal rights to all the powers concerned. For the disappearance of that concert, if it should disappear, it is obvious that the United States would not be responsible; but its disappearance would throw upon our government the necessity of considering the means by which the extensive interests that have grown up between our country and the East may be protected, preserved and extended. Our relation to this subject has been rendered more immediate than ever before by events growing out of the war with Spain —events so recent as to require no recapitulation or explanation.

We have with us this evening a distinguished diplomatic representative, who, though a native of the East, may, by reason of his experience, his studies, and his attainments be said to be at home also in the West. It was my pleasure not long ago to hold relations with him in his official character as Minister of China; and it is proper for me to confess that his excellent knowledge of English, while it greatly facilitated our intercourse, rendered me incapable of showing all the reciprocal courtesies which I should have been glad to bestow. An accomplished student of the laws and customs of nations, he is peculiarly well qualified to speak upon the subject on which he is to address us.

CHINA'S RELATION WITH THE WEST.

Address of the Chinese Minister, His Excellency WU TING-FANG.

We have all read about the dispute between two ancient knights over a shield, one claiming it to be gold and the other claiming it to be silver. The story is an old one, but the lesson it teaches is worth remembering. It is the failure to look at the other side of the shield that has given rise to all the misunderstanding in the intercourse between the East and the West. The different nations in the West have, within the present century, advanced so much in science, knowledge and wealth that it has become the fashion to speak of them as the most civilized nations on the face of the earth and to consider the nations in the East as much below them in civilization—in fact, as barbarous or semi-civilized. It has been too much the habit to ignore the good points the Eastern nations possess, and to leave out of account what they have done. This is hardly just. The East also has a civilization of its own. Of that civilization, China is the chief exponent. Among its achievements may be mentioned the invention of the mariners' compass, gunpowder and printing. It is not a civilization of mushroom growth. There is not a nation standing to-day that can trace its history as far back as China. She has witnessed the rise and fall of the ancient Egyptian Dynasties; the expansion of the Persian Empire; the conquests of Alexander; the irresistible advance of the Roman legion; the deluge of Teutonic hordes from the North; the dissolution of the Empire of Charlemagne; and the birth of all the modern nations of Europe. During the forty centuries of her existence there have gradually grown up institutions and laws adapted to the needs and character of the people; a literature as extensive and varied as that of ancient and modern Europe; a system of morality that can challenge comparison with any other the world has ever produced; and those useful arts that have never ceased to excite the wonder and admiration of the world. You may ask why Egypt, Persia, Greece, and even mighty Rome have successively succumbed to the ravages of time, while China alone has survived. The answer is not far to seek. It is the survival of the fittest. The working of this inexorable law of nature constantly weeds out those nations that cannot adapt themselves to the ever-changing conditions of life, and the fact that China is standing to-day shows conclusively that she has not outlived her usefulness to the cause of civilization.

Thus Chinese civilization has been weighed in the balance of time and not found wanting. But the conditions that have fostered that civilization have in recent years been greatly modified by steam and electricity. With the Himalayas on the west, vast deserts on the north, and large bodies of water on the east and south, China was a country extremely difficult to approach from all sides in days not very long ago. There she was left for centuries to work out her destiny practically free from outside influence and foreign molestation. But the steamboat and telegraph have changed the whole situation of things, and rendered it impossible for her to lead such a national life as she could before. It has taken her some time to awake to this fact. On this account, she has been called an unprogressive nation. This sentiment is voiced by Tennyson when he says,—
"Better fifty years of Europe than a cycle of Cathay."

But it is a mistake to think that China has been stationary. Compare China of the present day with China of fifty years ago, and the progress she has made will be at once apparent. There is a well-known law in physics that when a body is at rest or in motion, it will remain at rest or continue to move in a straight line unless acted upon by some outside force. This law holds good in the political as well as in the physical world. It is unreasonable to expect

China to break away from the long-established sway of custom in a moment. The inertia of centuries must be first overcome. The meeting of the Chinese and Western civilizations is a meeting of two social forces. We must look for the result not in the complete neutralization of one force by the other, but in the union of the two forces. It is the recovery from the shock of the collision that requires time. After the union of the forces is effected, movement in the resultant direction may be expected to be rapid.

Mechanics also teaches us that if the same force acts for the same period of time upon bodies of different masses, the velocity generated is inversely proportional to their masses. According to this law, when two balls, one weighing twice as much as the other, are thrown from the hand, the heavier one will go only half as far as the other. Now the population of the United States is estimated at 76,000,000, and the population of China is estimated at from 350,000,000 to 400,000,000, or about five times as large. We should expect, therefore, that a social or political movement, which would stir up the whole people of the United States, would, other conditions being equal, produce only one-fifth as much effect upon the people of China. But in order to obtain the same effect in China as in the United States, the force must be five times as great; or, if the force be the same, the time it is allowed to act must be five times as long. Thus for the apparently slow progress of the Chinese nation, we have a scientific explanation.

Though China may not have made very rapid progress from a Western point of view in times past, there are signs everywhere at the present day indicative of a general awakening among the people. We have already established a system of telegraphs which is now in operation in every province of China, and a message can be sent from one thousand miles in the interior to the furthest seaport in a few hours. With regard to the railroad, it was introduced in the north of China fourteen years ago, and I had the honor of being one of the promoters and directors that organized the first company. Since then it has been extended in different directions. A journey from Tientsin to Peking, which by boat would have taken three or four days a few years ago, can be accomplished now in a few hours. The grand trunk line from north to south is now being rapidly pushed forward, and in the near future a traveler from the extreme south of China will be able to go up by the "iron horse" to Peking in forty-eight hours. Such is also the case with water communication. We have steamers plying along the coast of China, and steamboats of light draught are seen on most of the navigable rivers.

It will be tedious to enumerate all the improvements that have been introduced within the last twenty or thirty years, but from what I have above indicated it is sufficient to show that China has not been napping. I do not say that all necessary reforms have been made, and I frankly admit that something more will have to be done. Our government and people are aware of this, and they are taking steps in that direction. But it should be remembered that it is not necessary to import by wholesale the Western civilization into China. What is suited to one country may not be suited to another. Wise statesmen do not rush forward to introduce new measures without serious consideration lest their introduction may cause disruption and harm not counterpoised by the good produced.

You have so many conflicting stories about China and the Chinese nowadays, that I must admit it is a difficult matter for anybody to distinguish what is true from what is false. Every globe-trotter, upon his returning home, generally has something to say about China, and is ever ready to give his impressions of the country and its people. A rocky hill may have the appearance of a sand dune on the outside. A passing observer is apt to mistake the one for the other. In order to find out the true character of the elevation, we must go below the surface. The same may be said of

China. The words of the globe-trotter must be taken *cum grano salis* with reference to all things Chinese.

The most important questions with which the Chinese Government has to deal arise from the spirit of commercialism and the spirit of proselytism. In all the treaties which China has concluded with Western Powers, there is an article generally known as the "Toleration Clause." This article provides in effect that Christianity inculcates the practice of virtue, and that those professing or teaching it should not be harassed or persecuted. This apparently innocent provision has not, however, helped to further the cause of Christianity in China. It must be borne in mind that this official recognition of Christianity was first obtained from her after a disastrous war. The clause was no doubt inserted with the best of intentions. But it had the apparent effect of exciting in the native mind the unfounded suspicion that a deep-laid political object was intended under the cover of religion. The provision itself was hardly necessary as the subjects of every Treaty Power are all protected under the general provisions which apply equally to missionaries. Unfortunately most of the troubles occurring in China have arisen from riots against missionaries. Hence it has been said by some foreigners in China that, without missionaries, China would have no foreign complications. I am not in a position to affirm or deny this.

But let us put the shoe on the other foot, and suppose that Confucian missionaries were sent by the Chinese to foreign lands with the avowed purpose of gaining proselytes, and that these missionaries established themselves in New York, Philadelphia, San Francisco and other cities, and that they built temples, held public meetings, and opened schools. It would not be strange if they should gather around them a crowd of men, women and children of all classes and conditions. If they were to begin their work by making vehement attacks on the doctrines of Christianity, denouncing the cherished institutions of the country, or going out of their way to ridicule the fashions of the day, and perhaps giving a learned discourse on the evil effects of corsets upon the general health of American women, it is most likely that they would be pelted with stones, dirt and rotten eggs for their pains.

What would be the consequence if, instead of taking hostile demonstrations of this character philosophically, they should lose their temper, call in the aid of the police, and report the case to the government at Washington for official interference? I verily believe that such action would render the missionaries so obnoxious to the American people as to put an end to their usefulness, and that the American government would cause a law to be enacted against them as public nuisances. Can it be wondered at then that now and then we hear of riots occurring against missionaries in China, notwithstanding the precautionary measures taken by the local authorities to protect them? It must not be understood that I wish to justify or extenuate the lawless acts committed by ignorant mobs, nor do I underestimate the noble and unselfish efforts of Christian missionaries in general who spend the best part of their lives in China. What I desire to point out is that the preaching of the Gospel of Christ in the interior of China (except with great tact and discretion) will, in the nature of things, now and then run counter to popular prejudice and lead to some disturbance.

The spirit of commercialism has lately risen to a dangerous pitch. As a market for the world's goods, China indisputably holds the first place, for the wants of 350,000,000 to 400,000,000 people have to be supplied in some way. It has been said that, as a market, one province of China is worth more than the whole continent of Africa. It has always been the policy of China to treat all foreign nations alike. They are all most favored nations in a literal sense. The maintenance of an "Open Door" is exactly in the line of her policy. But unhappily human nature is never contented. When a man gets an inch, he wants an ell. It is now the turn of missionaries to tell us that if there were no foreign adventurers in China there would be no foreign complications. Twenty-five centuries ago, our Sage Confucius, the greatest philosopher that ever flourished in China, said, "Wealth gotten by improper ways will take its departure by the same." This is equivalent to your proverb, "Goods ill-gotten go ill-spent." Nations as well as individuals should not forget this, as the maxim of Confucius as well as your proverb will always come true if any nation or individual should unjustly obtain possession of any property. Some people call themselves highly civilized, and stigmatize others as uncivilized. What is civilization? Does it mean solely the possession of superior force and ample supply of offensive and defensive weapons? I take it to mean something more. I understand that a civilized nation should respect the rights of another nation, just the same as in society a man is bound to respect the rights of his neighbor. Civilization, as I understand it, does not teach people to ignore the rights of others, nor does it approve the seizure of another's property against his will. It would be a sorry spectacle if such a glaring breach of the fundamental rights of man could be committed with impunity at the end of this nineteenth century. What would the future historian say when he should come to write about the events of this century? Is it not time that we should at least recognize the principle of righteousness, justice and fair play?

Mencius, a great philosopher of China, twenty-three centuries ago said: "I like life, and I also like righteousness; but if I cannot keep the two together, I will let life go and choose righteousness." Now, if people professing Christianity and priding themselves on being highly civilized, should still so far misconduct themselves as to disregard the rights of the weak and inexcusably take what does not belong to them, then it would be better not to become so civilized. It would be better to live amongst the people who practice the tenets of Confucius and Mencius than amongst a people who profess to believe in the highest standard of morality but do not practice what they believe. The aphorism of Tennyson should then be changed so as to read: "Better fifty years in Cathay than a cycle in Europe."

But I do not believe such practice of ignoring other people's rights is generally resorted to, and I am persuaded there are many people who denounce it. China welcomes to her shores the people of all nations. Her ports are open to all, and she treats all alike without distinction of race, color, nationality, or creed. Her people trade with all foreigners. In return, she wishes only to be treated in the same way. She wants peace,—to be let alone, and not to be molested with unreasonable demands. Is this unfair? She asks you to treat her in the same way as you would like to be treated. Surely this reasonable request cannot be refused. We are about to enter into the twentieth century, and are we to go back to the Middle Ages and witness again the scenes enacted in that period? I cannot bring myself to think that the world is deteriorating. I believe that in every country there are men and women of noble character—and I know in this country there are many such—whose principle is to be fair and just to all, especially to the weak, and that they would not themselves; nor allow their respective governments to commit acts of oppression and tyranny. It is such men and women that shed lustre on their respective countries. It is due to the noble and unselfish efforts of such good people that the scheme of a tribunal for the settlement of international disputes has been brought prominently before the world. May their grand scheme be soon carried into effect! The good such an institution will produce to the world will be manifold. All international disputes will then be settled in an amicable way without resort to arms and without bloodshed. There will be practically no more war. The blessings of peace will be permanent. Commerce and trade will be more steady and prosperous, and merchants will have more confidence in each other. All men will follow their respective avocations uninterruptedly. Nations will be brought into closer touch with each other, and their friendly relations will be more cordial.

These and many other beneficial results will, in my humble opinion, naturally follow from the establishment of an international court of arbitration. It is gratifying to hear that the project of a general disarmament, so nobly proposed by His Majesty the Czar of Russia and so readily seconded by the leading nations of the world, will soon lead to a conference. May it bear good fruit! May it be the precursor of an international court of arbitration! This is my earnest wish, and I am sure it is your wish and the wish of every man and woman who has the peace and well-being of the world at heart.

THE POLITICAL RELATIONS OF THE UNITED STATES WITH THE EUROPEAN POWERS IN THE FAR EAST.

LINDLEY MILLER KEASBEY, *Bryn Mawr College.*

His Excellency the Chinese Minister touches our tender points. The missionary, the tourist and the trader must certainly strike the conservative celestial as strange examples of Western civilization, and rather difficult to rate under his "Rules of Propriety." According to Mencius, the way to reach the hearts of the Chinese people is "simply to collect for them what they like and not to lay on them what they dislike." But this is not the way of the West; we propose to collect for them what we think they should like and lay on them what we like ourselves. A peculiar program perhaps, but in pursuance of such a plan the missionary, the tourist and the trader has each served his turn with some success.

True, Chinese civilization is very much older than ours, but we must not forget that in our youth we cherished the same childlike ideals. In the words of Jarric, the Jesuit historian: "If Plato were to rise from Hades, he would declare that his imagined Republic was realized in China." But against the advice of Aristotle, the Greeks themselves took to "retail trade" and in the brief course of our subsequent civilization, capitalism has all but encircled the globe. China is still uncontaminated, to be sure, but missionaries, tourists and traders have already inoculated her inert body-politic with the germs of Western commercialism, and let us hope rejuvenation will result.

There is a story of Chuang-tze, the Chinese Diogenes. He was fishing one day when two high officials approached him with the request that he undertake the administration of the state. Without turning his head Chuang-tze answered the envoys: "I have heard that in Ch'u there is a sacred tortoise which has been dead now some three thousand years, and that the prince keeps this tortoise carefully enclosed in a chest on the altar of his ancestral temple. Now would this tortoise rather be dead and have its remains venerated, or be alive and wagging its tail in the mud?" "It would rather be alive" replied the envoys, "and wagging its tail in the mud." "Begone," cried the philosopher, "I too will wag my tail in the mud." So China has been dead now some three thousand years and is weary of being venerated for her remains. She wants to wag her tail again, even though it be in the mud of Western civilization.

But knowing nothing of the incipient tail-waggings of the Chinese tortoise except from the reports of missionaries, tourists and traders, I will leave the discussion of this interesting problem to those who are better versed in the social anatomy of the celestials. We shall meet with others in the far East beside the Asiatics and the question arises: What effect will our present policy of expansion have upon our long-standing attitude toward the European powers?

We Americans are coming at the eleventh hour into the vineyard of Eastern politics. The earlier comers are murmuring somewhat against our sudden intrusion, it is true, but there is really no ground for complaint. We have certainly not been standing idle in the market-place, and if we are late in arriving, it is because we have had work to do in our own fields and a longer road to travel to the vineyard. And at all events—by analogy at least—we are entitled to the same reward as our European fellows who have borne the burden and heat of the day. We must not allow our equanimity to be in the slightest degree disturbed therefore by any lack in the cordiality of our reception.

Our own unpreparedness is a matter much more to the point. Coming by the unfrequented road from the West, we have had but little opportunity of learning the traditions of the place beforehand, and judged from the standpoint of our own experience the situation seems somewhat distorted. If of the many already called we hope to be of the chosen few, it will be well, therefore, before taking up our own burden to look about us a bit, lest we commit some silly blunder at the start difficult to retrieve.

Taken in its broader sweep, Western civilization is furrowed with the vicissitudes of conquest, but as far as our own experience goes, progress toward the West has been practically along an unimpeded path. This is due to the fact that inter-European competition was reduced to an earlier issue on this side of the globe, leaving independent republics, under the hegemony of the United States, in practical possession of the field. England has thus far been the only European power in any political position to dispute our exclusive claim to the New World, and under such extended territorial conditions contact might generate some friction, perhaps, but scarcely lead to controversy. The continent thus lay open to economic exploitation directly from the Atlantic, and, save for some trifling opposition on the part of the aborigines, American enterprise has consequently been afforded a fair field to run its full course to the Pacific. To us, therefore, expansion has merely meant a peaceful overland advance. But this is purely fortuitous, and it would not be the part of prudence to prognosticate the future from the precedents of so brief a past.

If our domestic traditions are then too limited to determine our present course, we may learn, perhaps, from the more extended experience of our foreign competitors. But in shaping our policy upon international analogy we must bear in mind that Europe and the United States are approaching the Asiatic problem from opposite points of departure— Europe from the East and the United States from the West —and each is accordingly inspired by a different set of ideals. European conclusions must consequently be applied with some reserve to the American side of the case; but if taken with proper precaution the analogy is sufficiently apposite.

The European current of commerce and colonization setting in toward the Pacific, differs from the corresponding course of Western civilization primarily in this: progress toward the East was originally confronted by compact native populations which caused the main stream to bifurcate, one branch proceeding across the northern plains of Siberia, the other reaching the South Sea by skirting the southern shores of the continent. Expansion across the desolate steppes in the North was unopposed save by unorganized aborigines, but the rich peninsulas and fertile islands of the South served each in turn as successive causes of international contention. European colonization in the East thus serves us with two sets of traditions, one evolved from a peaceful overland advance, the other proceeding from colonial controversy by sea. Russia's present political program is the outcome of the former, British imperialism is the result of the latter.

Our own progress across the plains and prairies of North America finds its closest European parallel in Russia's corresponding conquest of Siberia. Before both countries lay an immense extent of untilled territory, and the problem confronting each government has been to connect a far-lying frontier with a distant political base. Having succeeded in establishing our own transcontinental lines we can better estimate the importance of the Siberian railway and appreciate Russia's present endeavor to control an ice-free port on the Pacific. Russia's possessions in the far East constitute an integral part of her domain, just as the Pacific slope is included within our own body-politic. Russia's attitude toward China and Korea may, therefore, very properly be compared with our own rather ill-defined relations toward the Spanish-American states. In both cases it is a matter of border diplomacy rather than a question of colonial politics. In marking out a sphere of influence toward the south and in claiming certain exclusive privileges, Russia is accordingly following in our own footsteps and taking the same position in northern Asia that we have long since assumed in America. We should be careful, therefore, not to regard Russia's Eastern policy from the prejudiced standpoint of Europe. Her territorial position on the Pacific is entirely different from that of the other maritime powers, and much more closely akin to our own. We have always resented European interference in American affairs and Russia has consistently supported our claims. A sense of justice,—and to a certain extent also a feeling of gratitude,—should therefore, restrain us from joining in the indiscriminate European outcry against Russian aggression in Asia. So long as we believe in the protection of our own borders and jealously encourage reciprocity arrangements with our southern neighbors, we cannot consistently expect Russia to let down the bars and open her Pacific ports to the world. It is enough if she admit her friends, and if we continue to deport ourselves properly, we may doubtless always count upon a warm welcome within her gates.

Without prejudice to our cause we may, therefore, recognize the Russian ideal, and reckon upon at least one legitimate sphere of influence in northern Asia. Having definitely abandoned her earlier American enterprise, there is nothing, however, to attract Russia beyond her Pacific border. Herein we differ from our Slavic contemporary, for our missionaries long since led us to Hawaii and Dewey has recently established us in the Philippines. In thus transcending the limits of our continent, the Russian analogy fails; and among the islands of the South Sea we have recently come into contact with the other current of European colonization setting in along the southern littoral of Asia. We are here confronted with much more complex conditions, and it will be correspondingly difficult to discover the European counterpart of our policy. Fortunately for our purpose, however, international contest along this line has already resulted in a partial process of elimination, leaving England, the dominant naval power, in practical control. It is to Great Britain we may, therefore, look for further precedents in our present policy of over-sea expansion, as she is the only country which has successfully solved the problem of maritime colonization.

The influence of sea-power is a lesson we have already learned from English history. Let us hope, then, in applying our conclusions to the Pacific that we will at last realize the strategic importance of controlling the westerly trade-routes to the Indies, even as England has seen fit to place herself in possession of the easterly lines. Great Britain also affords us an admirable example of colonial administration, and sets us a civil service standard which we would certainly do well to emulate both at home and abroad. Up to the present, however, England being an industrial and the United States an agricultural country, the commercial cases of the two governments have not been at all analogous. Desiring to develop our manufacturing interests and subsist at the same time by exporting our raw materials, we have been unable to appreciate the universal advantages of the free-trade policy so ardently advocated by our leading competitor in the industrial field. And even now, when our infant industries are approaching maturity and need no further protection, we are still inclined to believe reciprocity will prove the better trade policy for us to pursue—at least with European and American countries. In Asia, perhaps, where the industrialists of Europe and America are meeting on common ground, the case may be somewhat different, but even here it would be a pity to become dogmatic and blindly follow any commercial creed until we are thoroughly cognizant of the situation.

Lord Beresford's pet policy of the "open door" will at best appeal to those established in the islands and along the southeastern littoral of the Asiatic mainland, whose primary aim is the economic exploitation of the continent. Germany and Japan should accordingly be in sympathy with the cause, and if properly persuaded, both powers may probably be induced to lend the doctrine their support. But French politics are proverbially problematic. To hazard a general proposition: extent of territory is usually more in keeping with France's conception of colonial success than the mere amount of revenue to be derived. Her domain being contiguous upon southern China, it is, therefore, very doubtful whether she will agree to abandon her present policy of encroachment for the doubtful benefits of the open door. And as for Russia, her case as we have already seen does not come within the category at all.

Thus upon our arrival in the far East we shall be met by at least two proposals; the sphere of influence and the open door. If importuned to make an immediate choice, we may best avoid the issue with the boy, who, when asked which hand he would have, laconically answered *both!* What we should object to is the alternative nature of the proposition; this endeavor on the part of the Europeans to draw us into their controversies and commit us to a particular cause. From our present position in the Philippines our immediate interests coincide, it is true, with the policy of the open door. The dismemberment of the Asiatic empire is not in other words to our advantage, and if we are wise we will continue to cultivate friendly relations with the Chinese with a view to encouraging reciprocal trade. We may well afford, therefore, to keep open house in our East Indian islands and vie with our neighbors in the measure of our hospitality. But our action in this particular case should not be supposed to commit us to the universal principles of free-trade. In Europe and America we must feel free to fall back upon reciprocity arrangements. Our relations with the Russians in northern Asia may likewise have to be regulated with similar formality, and it would be folly to antagonize our Slavic friends merely to inculcate an abstract doctrine, when equally good results are to be obtained by more politic means.

In short neither the "open door" nor the "sphere of influence" quite covers our commercial case. And yet our proclivities are sufficiently concordant with either policy to allow us to combine the benefits of both. We should recognize that the two doctrines are due to different sets of traditions and adapt ourselves accordingly to the divergent principles involved. If the Eastern camp is divided, it merely means that we shall have to treat with both parties. Coming alone from the West we are not diplomatically concerned with these time-worn controversies of the East, and we should find it comparatively easy, therefore, to preserve our traditional attitude of independence. We shall only have to insist upon regarding these questions of commercial policy from the relative point of view. If accused of inconsistency, we can then claim the privileges of an eclectic. To put it bluntly: our present part is to pacify Asiatics and not to contend with Europeans. Until we have adjusted our new burden, therefore, we had best adopt a policy of beneficent neutrality toward our foreign competitors. The Asiatic future is replete with economic opportunities which it were a pity to cloud with diplomatic complexities. Let us take Washington again as our guide: "The great rule of conduct for us, in regard to foreign nations, is in extending our commercial relations, to have with them as little political connection as possible." Or to paraphrase the words of Jefferson, let this be our motto in the far East. Commercial rivalry with all nations, political alliance with none.

THE REAL MENACE OF RUSSIAN AGGRESSION.

FREDERICK WELLS WILLIAMS, *Yale University.*

What we call the Far-Eastern Problem to-day is only an acute phase of the problem of the civilized races of mankind as it has been developed during many centuries. It is the eternal struggle of Turanian and Aryan, of East and West. In its larger meaning it is a contest between the exponents of autocracy and democracy, between absolutist and representative systems of rule; the conception of government under ancient tyrannies as opposed to modern individualism. In its especial relation to our own times it is the question as to which of these tenets of sovereignty is to be applied to the reconstruction of the effete empires of Asia, to the eventual control of civilized mankind. If, as Mr. Brooks Adams suggests, the velocity of the social movement of any community is proportionate to its energy and mass, and its centralization is proportionate to its velocity, the settlement of this problem of the ages may be near at hand. The time has already come when every live nation is necessarily concerned in its solution.

The evolution of modern Europe has involved the gradual elimination of small governments. Beginning with the absorption of feudal fiefs and the suppression of private war and brigandage, a process of concentration at natural centres presently developed a number of national groups which continued to incorporate and ingraft their weaker neighbors until only those remained who were allowed their autonomy because of the convenience or the jealousies of the great powers. The movement from a condition of physical dispersion to one of concentration has been going on from the break-up of the Roman Empire to the recent formation of a united Italy and a united Germany, nor is it possible to say that it has yet reached its limit.

This proceeding has assumed of late an aspect altogether at variance with its former manifestation, since the larger states have sought not only to add to their possessions in Europe but have reached out for colonies to exploit and to supply homes for their surplus populations. The process has in its recent phase been rendered feasible by two material agencies which have risen to predominant importance only within the century in which we live: these are modern fighting machinery and modern transporting machinery. The size and cost of military and naval armaments to-day place the means alike of attack and defence completely beyond the resources of smaller states; in precisely the same manner the introduction of artillery at the close of the Middle Ages, made the continuance of private warfare altogether too dangerous and costly a business for individuals and compelled the sovereign at once to police and protect his domain. The convenience and economy of this evolution are the best guarantees of its continuance until only those nations shall survive which are best fitted to administer the affairs and preserve the peace of the world. Have we any assurance that we have reached the end of a readjustment that has eliminated the names of Burgundy, of Savoy, and of Poland from the map of Europe, or that such existing survivals as Belgium, or Denmark, or Bulgaria are not destined sooner or later to follow in their train? The second agency, that of rapid travel and the transmission of information, renders it possible to administer territories which in the old days would have fallen apart from mere size and weight; also to convey orders and, if necessary, the troops to enforce them, over lands and seas which have heretofore offered insuperable obstacles to even the highest military and administrative genius. It is not easy to appreciate in a moment the enormous significance of a change in the conditions of life itself which removes us further from the time of Napoleon than he was—so far as means of transport and control of territory were concerned—removed from Alexander or Asshurbanipal. They had roads for the movement of armies by land and sailing vessels for their transport by sea; so had he, nor was his equipment for either element much more swift or certain than theirs. But within the past two generations an alteration in the mere mechanics of fighting and of government has carried us into a new world—a world differing effectually not alone in habits and ideals but in the foundations and instruments of its efficiency from those ancient and mediæval states which history offers as models.

These conditions are necessarily as yet so novel as to engender some vagueness of interpretation by philosophical speculators, some indefiniteness of purpose on the part of politicians. The main issues of this transition era with its measureless possibilities for the future are nevertheless at length grasped by the dominant statesmen of Europe. They begin now to understand that, given the control of sufficient resources, it is simply a matter of calculation how far the power of a single government may be extended over the peoples of the earth. Under present terms, moreover, those disabilities have substantially disappeared which formerly rendered the education and amalgamation of alien races brought under a common rule a hard and hazardous matter. Complete isolation and removal from prevailing influences are no longer practicable under normal conditions without artificial compulsion. The interchange of ideas proceeds inevitably and by itself throughout communities whatever their size and number. And as a corollary to this transfusion of intellectual life comes the inevitable employment for general purposes of the language in which instruction and information are disseminated. A secondary result, therefore, of prevalent tendencies is the spread of a few languages over the greater part of the world as the legal and literary media of the future, and the relegation of other tongues to the subordinate position of dialects which survive only as the vernacular of restricted districts.

Under widely varying circumstances and with numerous differences of detail Europe appears at the opening of the twentieth century to be entering upon a phase of its career somewhat similar to that which was marked by the establishment of imperial Rome nearly nineteen centuries ago. The machinery of the new centralization is certain to be more elastic as it will be more complex, the control will be less obvious and direct; but co-ordination of hitherto heterogeneous elements under some predominant power is apparently as inevitable and necessary now as it was then. In comparison with the vast extent of the new system the domain of ancient Rome shrinks to almost insignificant dimensions. The command of the habitable globe is for the first time in history possible to that power in whose hands are placed the resources that insure obedience, whose capital is the centre of exchanges. The area of its activities will embrace not Europe and the Mediterranean basin alone but the six continents and their outlying islands; its mastership must be exercised alike in all countries.

When we seek for the nation under whose ægis the rote and rule of old Rome may be resuscitated in the near future, only two appear as possible competitors for the great prize, the Slav and the Anglo-Saxon. These are the only races whose territories, and consequently whose potential strength in population and material resources, are adequate to the stupendous task, whose subjects are colonizers in the true sense that comprises both the peopling of waste spaces and the assimilation and subjection of foreigners to their institutions. These great rivals have been already long at work, each in characteristic fashion, fulfilling what we call, somewhat lightly perhaps, their manifest destiny, each a participator in the conquest of Asia. The solution of the problem seems to lie in their hands, and behind one or the other must sooner or later be ranged all the political forces of the world.

Superficially both of these colossal empires appear to denote the spirit of the West and all that this implies in the eternal opposition of Orient and Occident, to which allusion has been made. But the accidents of a capital located in Europe and an ancestry traced to a common Aryan origin must not mislead our conclusions. In temperament and propensity these two nations embody the same antagonism that has in times past ranged the civilized world in two hostile camps. Their pretensions are as diverse as those of Persia and Hellendom twenty-two centuries ago—when, too, Aryan chiefs focused and guided the ambitions of East as well as West to different ends. Russia, though arrayed in the panoply of Christendom and bearing the outward symbols of Western culture, is the embodiment and expression of Oriental absolutism, the synonym of obedience to a single will. Great Britain, the present leader of the Anglo-Saxon hosts, is the protagonist of Western conceptions of liberty and self-government. She stands for the freedom of subject as well of sovereign, which, being interpreted in terms made clear by generations of conflict between her own children, means the sovereignty of the subject, of the people. The principles upon which her constitution reposes are the result of centuries of education and evolution in which the races of the East have taken no part.

The past careers of these two aspirants for world-direction furnish a clue to what may logically be expected from them in the future. In the dawn of Slavonic history we find the ancestors of the Russians to be a wayward group of tribes unable to coalesce in effective federation until conquered and given the initiative by an alien power. What the Tartar Bulgars did for some of these clans in the lower Danube valley the Northmen of Scandinavia and the Mongols effected at different times upon other members of the race in Russia. The unity to which the Slavs could never of themselves attain was forced upon them from without; but they had their revenge in the end by absorbing their conquerors and reducing their organization to its simplest elements. From this the inference may not unreasonably be made that the Slavic type, though enduring, displays little administrative ability and yields inevitably to the higher political genius of others. It carries its arms far to-day, but its soldiers and colonists bear no new message to the Asiatics with whom they commingle. They overrun their waste places and change their manners and perhaps their language, but for government only offer a Western autocrat in place of an Oriental monarch. It is Asiatic absolutism again incarnate in an Aryan family, as in the days of the Medo-Persian dominion.

The Anglo-Saxon presents a striking contrast in every phase of this comparison. He compels submission not through mere numerical superiority or the primitive process of *force majeur*, but by reason of the inventive and organizing talent of the race. Never content with the experience and example of others, he has worked out his problems to his own satisfaction and impressed his conclusions as a logical necessity upon all with whom he associates. In the light of his past performances it is impossible to imagine that he can ever abandon his ideals or revert to the primitive principles of patriarchal rule. The inevitable outcome of the predominance of one of these two races in Asia is submission to the old-world dogma of divinely inspired sovereignty, of the other an attempt—it may be altogether in vain—to teach the subject the high doctrine of self-rule.

To these politico-historic considerations must be added the politico-economic aspects of the Eastern Question which are rapidly driving on toward a crisis. For the century that has so radically altered the national relationships in the civilized world has in equal degree revolutionized the economic situation. Mechanical appliances have increased production and facilitated the exchange of raw and manufactured materials out of all proportion to the increase in consumption and demand. A significant result of this transformation of the productive plant in the Western world has been the accumulation of enormous reserves of capital in the hands of the ablest members of civilized society. The demand of this capital for larger employment and the extension of its field of activity exerts a pressure upon the statesmen and legislators of Western nations absolutely irresistible in its effect. Within a score of years it has compelled them to explore and partition Africa and lay claim to even the minutest islands of the sea. But its grandest ambition must inevitably be devoted to enlightening the unregenerate populations of Asia and developing both the natural resources of their territories and the artificial appetites which will turn them into profitable consumers.

It is idle in face of a factor which is founded upon one of the strongest of human passions to argue the morality of this desire. Greed and fear have ever been, in one form or another, the two most powerful motives in history, and this predicament of modern times involves them both. For the stake is life or death; the nation that does not succeed in gaining at least a small share in this competition for new markets must succumb to a pressure that will surely annihilate. Yet the issue may none the less bring infinite possibilities for good to a vast aggregation of human beings who now lie fallow and inept to every quickening impulse. Evidently the happiness of many millions is to depend upon the outcome of a conflict which is both racial and industrial.

Applying these economic postulates to the two rivals which we necessarily keep in view, it remains to consider their relation to the problem before us. It is evident from what has already been adduced that political concentration is the order of the day, and that electricity, steam and steel are practical agents of the highest importance in the further prosecution of the struggle between East and West, because they make it physically possible for a single nation to conquer and rule the inhabited globe. This has never been the case before. In the past the contest between these diverse and dissenting parties has been unremitting; neither has been completely successful, and there has always been room for them both. The war was long and often fierce, but it could not be a war of extermination, for the defeated side could always flee to the barbarians beyond its remoter borders. Moreover, the unparalleled industrial evolution of the closing century has added a new element of gravity to the issue. If mechanical advantages render the extension of the struggle possible, this necessitates its spread; the first may be a matter of preference and policy, this is relentless natural law. The ancient ambitions of martial kings subside into insignificance when compared with the terrible earnestness of modern competition for industrial supremacy. This is the monstrous test of Nature herself to determine the fittest, one of those titanic cosmical throes wherein the individual and his desires disappear altogether in the immensity of the operation. Under antique influences, when even the smallest communities could subsist contentedly upon their own resources, it was feasible and sometimes profitable for nations to shut themselves within their own borders and stagnate behind the protection of fortified frontiers. To-day the action of commercial intercourse renders the policy of hermit nations odious alike to those without and to those within their boundaries. The industrial and trading portion of mankind insists upon adding to the area of its operations until every avenue to profit is opened and every people civilized. The strength and headway of this combination is such now that only a military colossus supported by sufficient troops and territories to sustain its own weight can presume to resist its continued expansion.

But what if such a colossus arise? What if the future unlike the past allow no space for two equally matched empires to contend without conclusion, if it provide no barbarian fastness as asylum for the defeated? Both contingencies may occur. The Colossus of the North, Antæus-like, is increasing his strength with each fresh contact with the soil; and already the exploitation of remote lands is leaving no territory untouched by the influence of economic laws that constitute producers of the same commodity, members of the same gild, wherever found.

Evidently the rivals approach the same goal from opposite directions and impelled by different forces. The manufacturing and trading nations advance upon hitherto unknown lands, moved by the silent action of a primary passion that transforms every qualified trader into the captain of a conquering host. It is not incredible indeed that the government which orders the foremost group of these commercial armies to-day may succumb to the lust of military power in the event of succeeding too rapidly. With the prize well in view England's temptation is perhaps the strongest and most subtle ever set before a nation, and her people and rulers are but human. But England herself is great only so long as as she leads her mighty offspring and expresses the racial idea. It is the natural tendency of her empire to fall away as its dependencies mature; the only real tie that binds the aggregation together is that of self-interest. The moment she goes counter, therefore, to this great aim of her coadjutors, the moment a scramble for spoils begins, her leadership is lost, the body and limbs separate. It has been her fate rather than her desire to add to her possessions great patches of barbarism in order to defend the preserves where civilization has already begun to replace ignorance and misrule. Her true course, however, is not annexation, but instruction; the operations of trade bring her victories more lasting than those won by Maxim guns; she has no need of a better ally.

Russia's objective, on the other hand, is international monopoly. Her tendency is toward increased centralization of authority and the concentration of aggressive power whose appetite for territorial extension becomes in the end a mania. There is no place in her schemes for countries that her garrisons do not occupy. To subvert in unending succession, to tax and oppress her subjects for the maintenance of the huge military machine—these are her aims, precisely as they were those of Darius long ago. They involve the suppression of the individual everywhere for the benefit of the ruler, the abasement of the subject, and the inevitable reduction of civilization to a level with the condition of purely military despotisms of the past. She cannot cease aggressions against her neighbors because she is powerless to change her ways and compete with those mercantile nations whose effective conquests are those of peace and the increase of plenty. She frankly and even cynically acknowledges her intention of pushing her acquisitions to the extreme limits of the continent upon which she has entered. She must do so: both to exercise those armies that may, if thwarted, turn and rend her, and to exclude forcibly from those vast spaces the agents of her insatiable commercial adversaries. The occupation of Manchuria by her troops and workmen under a contract with China which secures its complete segregation from the competition of outsiders is only the most recent instance of a policy she has applied wherever practicable. This last step, which excites considerable apprehension at the moment because her desire to cancel the Niuchwang railway contract might, if persisted in, threaten war with Great Britain, is especially interesting as demonstrating the inability of any Czar by himself to modify the national and dynastic program. Personally the present emperor is credited with a strong desire for peace; but it is impossible for him, however friendly his inclinations, to expose this natural outlet of his Siberian possessions to the free action of foreign business concerns before whose superior commercial ability Russian interests would inevitably decay. For Russian plans to succeed there must be monopoly and undisputed sway; the presence of a single interloper endangers the whole system. The Czar must, then, fulfil the family traditions and protect his children where they are confessedly incompetent to defend themselves, or forfeit the respect and endorsement of the army which is the foundation of his throne.

A melancholy reflection suggested by this incident is the fact that the greatest Russian sovereigns have always been the wickedest. A ruler there need only be callous enough to suffering and to breaches of the moral law to count to the uttermost upon the support of his fighting machine. The emperor who prefers the ways of peace, on the other hand, must defend his predilection against a hostile group of officers who, if they are convinced that rectitude is likely to be pushed far, can always replace him upon the throne with a more complacent instrument of their ambitions. The rift in the armor of Russia is the necessity, common to every despotism, of implicit reliance upon those to whom delicate and dangerous tasks are entrusted. Agents who are trained to the sort of business required by irresponsible monarchs will accept the death penalty for failure, they will not tolerate close scrutiny of their accounts. For this reason a habit of corruption has been fostered which the most strenuous absolutism in the world is powerless to keep in check. The vices of bribery and peculation are so generally recognized as prevailing everywhere in the Eastern world that we have come to attribute them, rather loosely and almost unconsciously, to climatic or geographical influences; yet the example of New Japan shows that they are not concomitants to life in the Orient, but are only inevitable to the Oriental system of rule. How deeply this disease of immorality has permeated their society may be inferred from the significant though horrible Russian adage that "Lord Christ himself would steal if his hands were not nailed fast to the cross."

Against these weaknesses in the body politic of Russia, however, may be balanced the vacillation inseparable to party government in Anglo-Saxon states, where waves of prejudice or sentiment not infrequently overwhelm and ruin the wisest plans of far-sighted statesmen. Though the Eastern power be less delicately adjusted for the great work of governing men it is less apt to be subjected to those strains which come from too strenuous a passion for righteousness. Nor, in this category of disabilities common to our race should we neglect those traits of timidity and selfishness which become the bane of purely commercial communities and finally sap their strength and invalidate their influence. Against this vital danger we of the West have ever need to be on our guard.

Such being the attitude and ability of these natural opponents it remains to consider their position upon the continent which is the arena of their struggle. Great Britain, with her present reserve of capital at home and her command of the sea, has the advantage of being able to strike wherever she chooses and strike with swift and terrible strength. But Russia, like the leviathan, having no vitals cannot be mortally wounded however severe the blow may be. With limitless numbers intrenched in her remote and unassailable strongholds she can neither be ousted from her possessions nor prevented from advancing. Though for the time being there is little advertisement of Western Asia in the newspapers it is not likely that she has abandoned her earlier intention of securing Turkey. Even Persia and India remain well within the horizon of her ambition. It is enough, she thinks, that the greater prize of China when won will secure the less. Meantime the Ottoman Empire, if shrewdly guarded against invigoration through European reforms, will ripen and then rot in iniquity so as to fall, helpless and inane, of itself into her lap. And the same is palpably true of Persia; while in India much more may be expected from the fermentation engendered by British philanthropy than could ever be won by Russian attacks. There are signs in that mysterious land of South Asia which seem to intimate that England's work instead of stimulating its inhabitants to learn the difficult lesson of self-control is exciting them to madness and revolt. It is only necessary, Russia concludes, to locate her frontier fortresses conveniently near and wait.

The end, therefore, is not yet. Much remains to be

achieved in order to perfect the instruments by which her plans are to be fulfilled, while the great distances which separate the different parts of the Russian Empire are covered with a network of railways, and its vacant spaces turned into breeding-places of armed men. Above all, it is essential to the completion of her purpose to secure that richest and most populous realm on earth which has hitherto escaped the hand of the despoiler. Russia's need of China does not at all imply a necessity for increased markets to satisfy the desires of an overflowing industrial population. It means the direct increase of her fighting force by the acquisition of millions of hardy peasants who can, under European training, be turned into admirable soldiers; it represents the addition to her already magnificent resources of the richest mineral deposits to be found anywhere in the world; it signifies to her manufacturing rival that these supplies of men and material are to be henceforth as in the past withdrawn from the general service of mankind and reserved for her exclusive benefit. With the immoderate power involved in the mastery of these possessions, extending over a wide and continuous domain, impenetrable from without, but made articulate within by methods which modern science provides, Russia will have only to issue commands while the inhabitants of the earth tremble and obey. For it must not be forgotten that her peculiar strength depends upon position as well as upon size. With her back to the frozen ocean and her feet planted firmly upon two continents, she occupies a strategic front that can be maintained against any assault. Add to this the natural wealth from the mines and fields and manual labor of Asia, and the result is a combination of potency and energy that not only defies attack, but eventually threatens destruction to every other existing political power. Upon the highlands of Central Asia have been bred in the past the races which overran and dominated the civilized West, and where these swarms were once raised other millions may spring up in the future to obey the call of the conqueror and spread devastation among those more cultured but less lusty peoples who represent our race. It might indeed be an interesting speculation to calculate the chances of Africa, Australia and the two Americas if pitted against a united Russian-Asia, in some supreme encounter a century or two hence. In actual fighting strength the sides might not be very uneven. But the result of such an estimate would be valueless, because no combination that could be imagined would bring all those diverse and unrelated continents together, while a true comprehension of every part and people of Asia under Russian leadership, as representative of her *Zeitgeist*, looms large from the obscurity that veils the coming age.

The future, then, admits a return to the conception of hermit nation only upon the condition that the hermit, like that great Assassin, Sheikh al-Jebal or the Old Man of the Mountain, be feared sufficiently to command implicit obedience from his instruments and inspire terror far and near among the nations. Only by sheer might and multitude of resources can he defeat the operations of those natural economic processes which diffuse prosperity and knowledge equally throughout the world. It appears to be not only evident but inevitable that Russia proposes to fill this fearful rôle of great reactionist. The strength and occasion for its exercise being granted, Russia with the confidence of a youthful and courageous savage intends to pursue her passion for omnipotence to the very end. A less rudimentary racial type would long since have been diverted from this artless ambition by the complex distractions of an inventing and speculative age; an older people would not have dared. In her indifference to the risk incurred, in the crudity of her ideals, in her deliberate preference for the ruthless way of the Ancient East, lie the menace of her pretensions. The conclusion to the contest already begun between Asia and Europe under Slav and Saxon leadership allows no alternative between victory on the one side and destruction on the other. Much is said at present of Russian alliances in Europe. It is eminently politic for her to secure as many of these as she may, provided they are to be had, as is usually the case, for the asking. The national bigotry and narrowness of decadent France seem to find in such a co-partnership some assuagement for recent mortifications; but Russia is of necessity equally opposed to all Western European states alike so long as they produce salable commodities and desire trade. Her friendships with some of them are only phases of a transition period while her plans await accomplishment, or are undertaken to divide the ranks of her enemies the more easily to overwhelm them. Permanent community of interests between such natural antagonists is as unlikely as was any lasting fellowship between the Roman Empire and its occasional barbarian allies. When she has won the prize set before her there will be no room left in the political firmament for luminaries of the second magnitude, no uncivilized regions, as of old, for the vanquished party to invade and settle, no long tension of inconclusive wars that retard growth indeed but leave the body of the nation free to pursue its accustomed vocations. Her victory will mean the sort of depressing monopoly which Napoleon sought to establish, but extended this time over a vastly wider sphere. Let us face the alternatives offered by this tremendous combat: they are either a crushing absolutism which must involve us all, or an era of prosperity brought about by a universalization of commerce unequaled hitherto in the world's history.

It is imperative to comprehend fully the purport of this great question and discern the abyss that yawns beyond. Nor is it necessary to defame the Russian character in order to strengthen the protest against their assumptions. It is in the race tendency rather than in the people themselves that the danger lies. They have often and beneficially played the rôle of civilizers in darkest Asia, enforcing peace and good order where none had been known for centuries. Their work in reducing the khanates of Turkestan and compelling the desert slavers there to forego their favorite activities of kidnapping and robbery, compares favorably with anything that England has done of the same sort. In dealing with the ruder Asiatic they undoubtedly succeed better than their less pliant rivals, the English; and by reason of the personal popularity of their administrators, as well as because of the prestige of their unbroken successes, they enjoy a fairer prospect of securing the guidance of militant Asia by choice of the fighting class than any other foreign folk. Yet it is this very *simpatica* with a grosser civilization than befits their Aryan descent that constitutes the gravity of the impending crisis. It shows that half-measures and a merely superficial modification of barbaric society satisfy the Russian conscience. It proves again, if additional proof be needed, that the Slav is ready in all that touches and inspires the soul of a nation to sink to the low level of Asiatic ideals, to surrender what he has learned from liberal Europe and relapse into the animalism and inertness of Oriental life. And when the mark of his European culture, brandished a little contemptuously now before our eyes, is at length thrown aside, we shall find ourselves, while opposed to this Caliban of to-day confronted with the old, unchanging issue of Eastern tyranny and retrogression *versus* Western freedom and progress.

To keep this protoype of brute force from pervading and controlling the whole world, the nations that still cherish lofty hopes for humanity must forget their sectionalism and stand together in battle. It is madness to abate one particle of the issue and declare that something ought to be conceded for the cause of peace, to pretend, as do some Englishmen already weary of the strain, that Russia if given Northern China, or Constantinople, or a port on the Persian Gulf, will be content. She is not striving for portions, but for the whole of Asia; when she has gained this she knows, and we must eventually agree, that nothing human can resist her. Fortunately for the cause of freedom America has just discovered that she is necessarily involved in the affairs of Eastern Asia; that she has a stake in common there with others whom she can already undersell in distant as well as in domestic markets; that her business compels her to join in the work of reducing barbarians to order and educating them; finally, and perhaps most fortunately of all for the present crisis, that there is no real antagonism between the mother-country and her once rebellious colony, but that friendly co-operation has only to be proffered to be eagerly accepted. When we realize that the menace of Russian aggression affects not only the political supremacy of Great Britain in Asia but the free exercise of those high aspirations which are vital to the existence of every regenerate people, we will cease to imagine vain fears of imperialism and assemble the utmost strength of the enlightened West against that portentous imperialism embodied in the spirit of a devouring and devastating East. Finally, when we appreciate the fact that to secure China is the *sine qua non* of Russian designs for the establishment of a universal empire, that without her wealth and willing hands the Muscovite can never become master of a double continent and so of the world, we will listen before it is too late to the Macedonian cry of that misgoverned nation to go over and help them.

Appendices.

I. THIRD ANNUAL MEETING

OF THE

American Academy of Political and Social Science.

"THE FOREIGN POLICY OF THE UNITED STATES: COMMERCIAL AND POLITICAL."

Report of the Committee on Meetings.

Two years ago when the Academy decided to inaugurate a series of annual meetings it was felt by your Committee that the value of papers discussed at such meetings would be greatly increased if grouped about one subject. In this way the best thought and experience of the country could be concentrated upon definite public questions. Each year would thus mark an important contribution to the literature of political and social science.

The success of the Third Annual Meeting has fully justified the expectations of the Committee. The concentration of public attention upon the questions connected with our foreign policy together with the high authority of those who took part in the discussions, placed the meetings prominently before the eyes of the public. The information accessible to the general public on the great public questions confronting the country was to be found, in the main, in the newspaper press. Colored as this information was by partisanship, all thoughtful citizens were anxious to obtain trustworthy information and to receive the benefit of unprejudiced opinion.

In planning a thoroughly scientific examination of our commercial and political policy, the Committee feels that the Academy has rendered a real service, not merely to its members but to the country at large.

The plan for the annual meeting included four scientific sessions, held on the afternoon and evening of Friday and Saturday, April 7 and 8, together with a visit to the Commercial Museums Saturday morning, April 8. The afternoon sessions were held in the Assembly Room of the Manufacturers' Club and were largely attended.

The session of Friday afternoon, April 7, which was devoted to a discussion of the "Government of Dependencies," was presided over by Professor Samuel McCune Lindsay, of the University of Pennsylvania. In introducing the speakers Professor Lindsay emphasized the fact that the committee in charge of the meeting had but one end in view—namely, the impartial discussion of greet public questions. The diversity of opinion evoked by the discussions fully corroborated the statement of the presiding officer.

On Friday evening, April 7, the Honorable Carl Schurz delivered the annual address on "Militarism and Democracy." Professor E. J. James, of the University of Chicago, and president of the Academy, presided, and in his opening remarks commented on the work of the Academy, past and present, and mapped out its future field of usefulness. The remarks of the president are printed in full in another portion of this volume.

On Saturday morning, April 8, the members of the Academy were invited to visit the Commercial Museums, where Dr. W. P. Wilson had arranged a special exhibit of products of the far East. This visit proved one of the most interesting events in connection with the annual meeting. The care and skill with which the exhibit was arranged gave to the members the possibility of acquainting themselves at first hand with the economic resources of the East. In a few well chosen remarks Dr. Wilson pointed out the possibilities of trade and commerce and explained to the members the organization and work of the museum.

The session of Saturday afternoon, April 8, was devoted to a discussion of "Our Commercial Relations with the far East," Professor Roland P. Falkner, of the University of Pennsylvania, in the chair. Both Mr. Ford's and Mr. Hill's papers presented a wealth of material on this important question.

The discussion of Saturday evening on "Our Political Relations with the far East," proved one of the most interesting of the series. The presence of four distinguished speakers attracted one of the largest audiences in the history of the Academy. The addresses of all the speakers, particularly that of his excellency, the Chinese minister, Wu Ting-fang, were received with great interest.

That the discussions of the annual meeting attracted wide-spread attention was attested by the great number of editorial comments in newspapers of all sections of the country. The early publication of the proceedings will give to the members of the Academy who were not able to attend the meeting the opportunity of profiting by the material presented.

Your committee arranged for a number of social events in connection with the annual meeting. On Friday evening, April 7, a reception was tendered by the Academy to the Honorable Carl Schurz, which gave to our members the opportunity of meeting the distinguished guest of the Academy. On Saturday afternoon, April 8, Mrs. Talcott Williams entertained the members at her home and gave them an opportunity to meet his excellency, the Chinese minister. On Saturday evening, April 8, the University Club tendered a reception to the Chinese minister, the Honorable John Bassett Moore and the other speakers at the annual meeting.

The committee on meetings takes this opportunity to

express to the president and directors of the Manufacturers' Club, the president and board of governors of the University Club and to the director of the Commercial Museums, Dr. W. P. Wilson, their appreciation of the courtesy of these organizations in co-operating with the committee in the arrangements for the meeting.

The expenses of the meeting, which would have proved a very serious financial burden to the Academy, were defrayed by a special committee of fifteen members, each of whom contributed fifty dollars to the special fund. The members of the committee were: George Burnham, George Burnham, Jr., Andrew Carnegie, John H. Converse, Edwin S. Cramp, Samuel Dickson, W. W. Frazier, Charles C. Harrison, Samuel F. Houston, Theodore Marburg, John D. Rockefeller, J. G. Rosengarten, Charles A. Schieren, Isaac N. Seligman, John Wanamaker. This fund was supplemented by a number of subscriptions from ten to twenty-five dollars, contributed by the following gentlemen: Oliver H. P. Belmont, Charles J. Bonaparte, Henry E. Busch, Clarence H. Clark, Dr. J. M. DaCosta, Hon. George F. Edmunds, Theodore M. Etting, Abram S. Hewitt, Thomas McKean, Jr., Robert C. Ogden, Charles E. Pugh, Charles Richardson, Gustav H. Schwab, M. Hampton Todd, Harry F. West, George Wood.

To the members of the special committee, as well as to the subscribers, your committee on meetings desires to extend its sincere thanks.

      Respectfully submitted,
        L. S. ROWE,
         Chairman.

ROLAND P. FALKNER,
SAMUEL MCCUNE LINDSAY,
E. R. JOHNSON,
L. S. ROWE,
 Committee on Meetings.

II.

INTRODUCTORY ADDRESSES OF THE PRESIDENT OF THE ACADEMY, PROFESSOR EDMUND J. JAMES, OF THE UNIVERSITY OF CHICAGO.

THE AMERICAN ACADEMY AND ITS WORK.

Remarks at the Evening Session of the Annual Meeting, Friday, April 7, 1879.

Members and guests of the Academy: Before the time set for another annual meeting comes around, our association will have completed its first decade. On the fourteenth of next December the Academy will have been in existence ten full years. It would seem to be appropriate, therefore, on an occasion like this to cast a brief glance back over the history of our organization and possibly cast a brief horoscope of its future.

One element of success in the work of the Academy is to be found in the comparative permanence which has been secured in the general management of affairs and in the issue of our publications. Our present Advisory Committee, which has been a great help to us in our work still contains the names of many members who were on the committee when it was first organized. The losses from this committee have been few though serious. The distinguished economist, Francis A. Walker, the distinguished constitutional authorities, Judge J. A. Jameson, and the Honorable Thomas M. Cooley were lost to the Academy by death. The addition of such men as the Rt. Hon. Lord Herschell, whose sudden death, however, deprived us so soon of his assistance, and the Rt. Hon. Arthur J. Balfour, the very Reverend John J.

Keane, D. D., and other eminent men, have brought to our councils, added wisdom and strength.

The present Editor in Chief of the publications of the Academy, Professor Roland P. Falkner, of the University of Pennsylvania, was one of the associate editors when our work was first inaugurated, and has furnished, therefore, the continuous element in this important branch of our work.

I see around me still nearly all the men who were active in the original planning of the Academy with the exception of the lamented Brinton Coxe. I am especially pleased to see here to-night—I know that you will pardon me this personal allusion—and I trust that he will also, my friend Mr. J. G. Rosengarten, a man to whom this Academy owes very much, as do indeed, so many other of the successful organizations for public work in this city. It was Mr. Rosengarten who brought to the aid of the Academy in the very first instance the name and the prestige of the old Philadelphia Science Association, an organization which had done a useful and honorable service in this community. Without the assistance of Mr. Rosengarten at this juncture it is a serious question whether the Academy could have been organized on the liberal scale which was actually adopted. He has been ever since one of the quiet, unostentatious, most important elements in our work.

Dr. Lindsay will, in a few moments give you some detailed account of the actual work of the Academy during the last year.

To the larger aspects of our work as seen from the point which enables us to look back over a full decennium, I would briefly call your attention. When the Academy was organized we set before ourselves a number of tasks. We undertook to initiate and carry out various lines of scientific and practical activity. We proposed to secure, if possible, a large membership, believing that in this way we should secure for our publications a wider and more extensive influence. We undertook to hold regular meetings of the

Academy for the reading of scientific papers and for the discussion of scientific matters. We held out the prospect that these papers and such other material as we might find valuable, should be published in the form of a regular serial. We expressed the hope that we should be able to collect a library, and that we might be enabled, as the years went on, to undertake special investigations under the immediate auspices of the Academy itself, which might in this way assist in the development of certain work, which would not otherwise be feasible.

It is, of course, too much to expect that in a large plan of this sort we should be able within the short period of a single decade to even initiate all these various departments of work, to say nothing of carrying to complete development any one of them. But a glance at our history certainly shows that we have at least made a beginning in nearly all of these directions, and in some of them have carried out very fully, as fully as might be reasonably expected under the circumstances, the program which we announced.

We have to-day, as you learn from our printed announcements, a membership including subscribing members, of nearly two thousand. This is surely a satisfactory fulfillment of our undertaking to secure a large membership. No other body similar to ours working in these fields has anything like the same number of members. And while a large membership is not by any means the only test of the value of such an organization, it is at any rate a proof that the work it is doing commands a certain general sympathy and support among thoughtful people here and elsewhere. It is interesting to know that the membership is not limited to citizens of Philadelphia, or of Pennsylvania, or even of the United States, but that a very large proportion, something like 10 per cent, are to be found in foreign countries. Great Britain, France, Germany, Holland, Switzerland, Italy, Spain, Russia, South and Central America, China, India and Japan have representatives in our body.

We have held regular meetings, either monthly or quarterly, since the organization of the Academy, and during the last three years we have inaugurated a special annual meeting similar to the one which we open to-night for the purpose of discussing more in detail, than would otherwise be possible, some question of important theoretical or practical bearing. We are now publishing the thirteenth volume of our proceedings, and I think no one can examine these publications without being convinced that they form a substantial contribution to the development in theoretical and practical directions of the political and social sciences. We have collected a few books which may form the nucleus of a library, and we stand ready to inaugurate the work of special investigation as soon, and carry it as far, as any special funds given to the Academy for that purpose may justify.

The outlook, therefore, is extremely promising for the work of the next decade, and I should like simply to present one thought for your consideration on this occasion, and that is the desirability of securing as soon as may be convenient a suitable building, properly equipped and prepared for the special work of the Academy. We have thus far been compelled to utilize for our work such quarters as we might be able to obtain from time to time, hiring usually special rooms for our public meetings.

I think it is due to express in a public way the appreciation of the Academy for the courtesy which the University of Pennsylvania has shown to this organization from its beginning in practically putting at its disposal, free of charge, a room in the University building for the conducting of certain portions of its work. It is not easy to see how in early days we could have inaugurated our work at all had it not been for the generous attitude of the University toward our society.

When the Academy was organized in the first instance I maintained that the headquarters should be located permauently in the city of Philadelphia. It was natural that some persons should have thought that my argument found its chief support in the fact that I was then living in the city of Philadelphia and connected with the University of Pennsylvania. But my experience in the work of the Academy during the ten years since its organization has amply borne out my views at that time. And now that I can look at the work from a view-point a thousand miles away, I am still more fully convinced that the city of Philadelphia was the only city in the United States in which the work could have been begun as it was, and could have reached its present proportions within such a brief period.

Philadelphia is *par excellence* the home of the learned society. You have the American Philosophical Society, the oldest and still the most respectable of these organizations. Founded by Benjamin Franklin, the father of so many excellent things in this city and country, it has done a wide and useful work, and Philadelphia and the whole country may be proud of its career.

In the Academy of Natural Sciences you have another organization whose work is known wherever scientific men are prying into the mysteries of the universe.

In the Franklin Institute there is still another organization of the same kind, which has done in the department of engineering a work very similar to that accomplished by the Academy of Natural Sciences in its own proper field.

In the Pennsylvania Historical Society you have an organization and an equipment, which in its publications and series of contributions to American History is certainly not surpassed by any other similar organization in the United States, and equaled by few.

Surely all these things point to the fact that here was the proper place for such an organization, and the experience of the last ten years, though brief and partial, has amply sustained this view.

There is another favoring circumstance here, in the existence of the University of Pennsylvania, and its past close relations to the work of such an organization as this. To the work of an academy of political and social sciences which is to be fruitful, permanent and far reaching the aid of a great institution of learning in which due attention is given to the cultivation of this field, is almost absolutely necessary. The University of Pennsylvania has made wonderful strides in the last few years toward a leading position among the great American universities, and in no department has it done more or achieved a greater success than in that of the political and social sciences. I say it after a due deliberation and with a pretty full knowledge of existing facilities for the study of these subjects in the United States, that nowhere is to-day a better opportunity offered for the advanced student to get the kind of help which he needs in the prosecution of his studies in the field of the political and social sciences than in the University of Pennsylvania. Such a department is of enormous aid in the proper development and management of the work of a society like our own.

Here then the conditions are favorable for our work as shown by the best of all tests, the success which has attended it.

We are now about to enter upon the second decade, and I believe that the next great step for us to take is in the direction of securing an adequately equipped building which may serve as the headquarters of the work of the Academy, where its administrative work may be done with suitable accommodations for its library, which will enable us to make it more useful to the members and to the general public as well, and with suitable halls for its meetings, and with the opportunities for special investigation and research which the advanced student or college or university professor needs. The existence of such a building as this, would, I am sure, mark a new era in the history of the Academy and render permanent the achievements which have been thus far effected, opening the way for new advances in many different directions, now only slightly appreciated, and perhaps not even yet dreamed of.

To the fullest and most complete working of human forces there belongs not merely a soul, but a body. We have been evolving a soul—if you may permit us to use such an expression—during the first ten years of the existence of the Academy. The time has come to clothe that soul with a body. A sound mind in a sound body, a beautiful soul in a beautiful body. This is our desire and expectation.

It is permitted to young men to dream dreams and old men to prophesy. As I stand half way between youth and old age I may be permitted to take advantage of the privileges of both, and dream a dream and prophesy a prophecy.

I dream of the time when the Academy will be properly housed here in this city in such a building as I have indicated, equipped with special funds for carrying on special investigations similar to those which enable the Academy of Natural Sciences to organize its expeditions; the Franklin Institute to organize its expositions, and the Historical Society and the Philosophical Society to do their appropriate work. A building which will enable us to accumulate a special library along lines not cared for by existing institutions, and which will enable us to offer these facilities in the freest and fullest way to the public is a necessity.

I prophesy that long before we shall have completed the second decade of our existence such a building will be constructed and in use. I bespeak for this project your hearty sympathy and interest, and your co-operation in exciting and developing such an interest among the public spirited citizens of Philadelphia as will enable us to carry out this project in the fullest and most satisfactory manner.

INTRODUCING HONORABLE CARL SCHURZ.

MEMBERS AND GUESTS OF THE ACADEMY:—It is *par excellence* the function of a society like ours to bring to the discussion and consideration of every public question that patient and open mind which is characteristic of the true scientific man. It is our duty to see that, so far as possible, all sides of important public questions shall receive due attention and thought. Our attitude toward all questions, no matter how practical they become, is that of the scientific mind, pure and simple. The Academy, as such, can take no side upon any concrete public question. It can, as such, espouse the cause of no party; its sole purpose is to elicit truth upon all questions falling within the general field to the cultivation of which it is devoted. I may be mistaken, of course, but I think that just at this juncture in our country we need especially to develop this attitude of mind; that just at this time we ought to apply the cold and impartial test of scientific reasoning, so far as possible, to the important concrete questions which are attracting so powerfully our attention.

Our newspapers, as a rule, even when they have upon their staffs men properly qualified to discuss these questions, do not allow them an opportunity to express their free and unbiased opinion. But having taken sides upon a public question; having determined that they will espouse the policy of one party or another; that they will espouse or oppose the President or other political party leader, every man in such an office is compelled to prostitute his talents in order to advance and represent the views of his paper, no matter how much they may be opposed to his own personal views. Whatever may be said of the legitimacy of such a system it is certainly not calculated to give an opportunity for the free and uninterrupted play of individual opinion. And as our newspapers are nearly all under the power of one or another illegitimate influence, looking at them from the standpoint of public interest, we have almost ceased to have the kind of free and impartial discussion of public questions which it lies in the interest of the democracy to promote.

Under these conditions the average citizen is oftentimes at a serious loss to know exactly what the facts are in regard to any particular subject—still more at loss to know upon whose honest and independent judgment he may, to some extent, rely. We have had no better illustration of this than the attitude of the newspapers toward the Spanish war, and toward the Philippine embroglio which has grown out of that. If a newspaper has made up its mind to support the policy of the government, whatever that policy might turn out to be, it has had only foul epithets, or at least the most evil and unfair criticism for any one who was inclined to raise the question, whether this subject ought to be more fully discussed before it was settled, or whether we ought to consider the question at least in all of its aspects and try and settle it in the thoughtful way rather than by mere haphazard.

As said before, the Academy takes no attitude upon these and similar questions. It is neither for nor against the policy of the United States in the Spanish war. It is neither for nor against the policy of the President in the Philippine matter, but it is profoundly interested in securing a fair and full discussion of these questions in all their various ramifications.

We are fortunate to-night in having with us a gentleman who has distinguished himself throughout his career for independence of judgment and plain speaking. He has spoken the truth as God has given him to see the truth, without fear or favor. He has had experience in almost every line of public service in the United States. He has seen our politics and our administrative system from every point of view. His opinions, therefore, whether in our opinion sound or not, have the advantage of being based upon a long experience and an extensive knowledge of men and things. He has filled many positions of public trust, and has graced them all. He has discussed many subjects of public policy, and has illuminated them all. We are glad that in the presentation of one aspect of this important question before the American public, we have a man of such ability and of such straightforward honesty to present, what it is true, may be only his own views, and with which we may not agree, but which will have the great advantage of being the honest and outspoken and the uninfluenced views of an experienced public man.

I cannot drop this subject without making one more point which we Americans are sometimes apt to lose sight of. We are aware, of course, of the great influence of the foreign element in our midst We know what opportunities we have offered to the foreigner. We realize to some extent what he has done for us. The immigrant of the last two generations has built our railways, has dug our canals, and has settled up our unoccupied territory, and has helped us fight through one of the great civil struggles of our history.

All this we recognize, all this we appreciate, but I am afraid we do not always recognize so fully what contributions the same class of people have made to the ideal sides of our life. And in the career of the gentleman who is to address us this evening we have a striking illustration of the service which the educated, thoughtful foreigner may do for the higher sides of American life. Mr. Schurz has stood from the beginning of his career for the best things, and for the emphasis of the best things in American politics. He comes from a country with whose form of government and political institutions Americans have as a rule very little sympathy, but he has demonstrated in his own career how a man may be thoroughly devoted and patriotic to the best interests of the German people, and at the same time one of the most devoted and patriotic of American citizens. We may well be proud of the fact that such a career as that of Mr. Schurz's is possible in the United States, and be grateful that men have been found strong enough to run it.

I take great pleasure in introducing to you the Honorable Carl Schurz who will address you on the subject of "Militarism and Democracy."

THE EAST AND THE WEST.

Introductory Remarks on the Political Relations of the United States with the Far East, at the Evening Session, Saturday, April 8, 1899.

Professor JAMES:—Members and guests of the Academy: Dr. Charles C. Harrison, provost of the University, who had kindly consented to preside this evening, begs to be excused on account of a severe cold, which has deprived him temporarily of the use of his voice.

I think those of us who have lived during the last decade of this century must congratulate ourselves that we have been living in one of the most interesting periods, not only of the last hundred, but of the last three hundred, or even of the last five hundred years. We can take up no newspaper in these days without finding something which reminds us that we are a part of the great world which has its limits no longer in the civilized life of Europe and the nations which were the outgrowth of that, but which extends to the uttermost confines of the globe and includes practically to-day, as never before in the history of the world, the whole human race. The astonishing developments in all parts of the earth, which owing, among other things to the steam-engine and the telegraph, have become a part of our daily information and our daily interest, have brought us together and made us feel the solidarity of the whole human kind in a way quite unparalleled at any previous time.

I am inclined to think that when the historian of this century comes to describe the great events which have taken place within it he will find nothing more significant and more important in the great events which will follow in the next and in the succeeding centuries—nothing which will be, in his opinion, more remarkable than the new contact of the Orient and the Occident. There is nothing of deeper significance in the Napoleonic campaigns, or in the struggle for the reconstruction of Europe beginning in 1848 and ending in 1871, or in our own great struggle for national unity, or in the brief conflict which marked the passing of Spain as a great colonial power,—I say in none of these events is there a more important significant prophetic element than in the awakening of Japan and China and of the ever hastening process of union between the East and the West.

We are fortunate in having with us for the discussion of the question which the Academy has selected for this evening's session, namely, "The Relations of the East and the West" a group of men who are competent to speak on this topic, as perhaps no other equal group of men to be found in this country.

In the first speaker we have a distinguished member of the Academy who is known by reputation to the entire country, and whose career has been an honor to the profession to which he belongs. He has in his own work afforded us a striking example of the all-compelling power of expert knowledge and ability even over political partisanship and political influences which would gladly have managed things alone if they could have done so.

The political authority of the country in our last crisis was compelled at more than one time to call upon the patient and thorough knowledge of the scholar, and in no case was this policy more profoundly vindicated than that of the Honorable John Bassett Moore, of Columbia University, who will open this discussion.

www.ingramcontent.com/pod-product-compliance
Lightning Source LLC
Chambersburg PA
CBHW031826230426
43669CB00009B/1242